The Ultimate Spelling List (Book 2):

Most Common and Important Spoken and Written Words In English

\- Comprehensive Daily Practise Word Lists For Primary & Lower Secondary School -

Shenouda Makarie

Lifelong Education

1st Edition
2017

Makarie, Shenouda
The Ultimate Spelling List (Book 2): Most Common and Important Spoken and Written Words In English. Comprehensive Daily Practise Word Lists For Primary & Lower Secondary School

National Library of Australia Cataloguing-in-Publication entry
Creator: Makarie, Shenouda, author.
Title: The ultimate spelling list : most common and important spoken and written words in English : comprehensive daily practise word lists for primary and lower secondary school. Book 2 / Shenouda Makarie.
ISBN: 9780994283658 (paperback)
Target Audience: For primary school age.
Subjects: English language--Orthography and spelling--Problems, exercises, etc.--Juvenile literature. English language--Orthography and spelling--Study and teaching (Primary) Spellers--Juvenile literature.
Dewey Number: 372.632

First Printing: 2016
ISBN 9780994283658

Lifelong Education Series
Other Titles available:
- The Ultimate Spelling List (Book 1): Most Common and Important Spoken and Written Words In English
- Times Tables (Book 1): Comprehensive Memorisation Program with Exercises, Tables 1-6
- Times Tables (Book 2): Comprehensive Memorisation Program with Exercises, Tables 7-12
- Multiplication & Division (Book 1): Comprehensive Mental Exercises, Tables 1-12

Sydney, NSW 2000 – Australia
books@lifelongeducation.com.au
For enquiries or further copies of this book, visit: www.lifelongeducation.com.au

CONTENTS

INTRODUCTION

These days more than ever it is difficult for parents, teachers and tutors to create word lists that are both relevant and important to a child. The spelling words included in this book are **carefully researched and selected from a large worldwide, genre-balanced and up-to-date corpus of contemporary English** – reflecting the **most common and important** spoken and written words in the English language.

This is an incredibly powerful tool! It will enable children to quickly build up a vocabulary that is sound and highly relevant. All in all, these word lists will assist in developing comprehension and communication skills in English.

Beautifully laid out and set out over **2 volumes with 4,800 words**, both books contain comprehensive daily practise **word lists** for primary and lower secondary school children. Children are encouraged to look up the meanings and usage of the words in the dictionary to further enhance their learning.

Daily practise, repetition and structured exposure to new words are critical in helping improve a child's spelling and vocabulary throughout their primary years.

To get the most out of this book, ensure your child completes in order,
at least one set every week, practising daily.

Take charge now, and with the help of these unique comprehensive books, your child will reap the benefits throughout their school years and beyond!

Happy learning,

Shenouda Makarie

SET 1

Date: ....

Word List

dramatically	**mentally**	**imagination**	**southeast**	**parking**
essence	**coastal**	**constitute**	**thousand**	**shooting**
extension	**maintain**	**segment**	**interact**	**reporter**

INSTRUCTIONS: Review the word list above and then cover. Have someone read out each word while you write them in the spaces below. Review any misspelt words 3 times.

LOOK. SAY. COVER. WRITE. CHECK.

Practise

Practise 1

Practise 2

Practise 3

TIP Remember, look up each word in your dictionary to learn its meaning!

Need extra practise?
Printable blank practise sheet available from: www.lifelongeducation.com.au/spelling_practise_sheet
(also available on page 167)

SET 2

Date: ....

Word List

serious	**identity**	**interrupt**	**massive**	**consciousness**
gesture	**climate**	**province**	**towards**	**transform**
database	**convince**	**musical**	**bombing**	**appreciation**

INSTRUCTIONS: Review the word list above and then cover. Have someone read out each word while you write them in the spaces below. Review any misspelt words 3 times.

LOOK. SAY. COVER. WRITE. CHECK.

Practise

Practise 1

Practise 2

Practise 3

TIP Remember, look up each word in your dictionary to learn its meaning!

Need extra practise?
Printable blank practise sheet available from: www.lifelongeducation.com.au/spelling_practise_sheet
(also available on page 167)

SET 3

Date: ....

Word List

calculate	**conference**	**expense**	**multiple**	**traditionally**
theater	**traditional**	**scratch**	**constant**	**opposite**
dynamic	**invasion**	**narrative**	**meantime**	**quality**

INSTRUCTIONS: Review the word list above and then cover. Have someone read out each word while you write them in the spaces below. Review any misspelt words 3 times.

LOOK. SAY. COVER. WRITE. CHECK.

Practise

Practise 1

Practise 2

Practise 3

TIP Remember, look up each word in your dictionary to learn its meaning!

Need extra practise?
Printable blank practise sheet available from: www.lifelongeducation.com.au/spelling_practise_sheet
(also available on page 167)

SET 4

Date: ....

Word List

measurement	**regardless**	**apartment**	**sensitivity**	**suffering**
protection	**particular**	**immigrant**	**inquiry**	**helicopter**
exciting	**sometimes**	**discover**	**personality**	**alcohol**

INSTRUCTIONS: Review the word list above and then cover. Have someone read out each word while you write them in the spaces below. Review any misspelt words 3 times.

LOOK. SAY. COVER. WRITE. CHECK.

Practise

Practise 1

Practise 2

Practise 3

TIP Remember, look up each word in your dictionary to learn its meaning!

Need extra practise?
Printable blank practise sheet available from: www.lifelongeducation.com.au/spelling_practise_sheet
(also available on page 167)

SET 5

Date: ....

Word List

educational	**expansion**	**refugee**	**envelope**	**concerned**
sentiment	**possess**	**gentleman**	**soldier**	**warrior**
trouble	**audience**	**precise**	**statute**	**quickly**

INSTRUCTIONS: Review the word list above and then cover. Have someone read out each word while you write them in the spaces below. Review any misspelt words 3 times.

LOOK. SAY. COVER. WRITE. CHECK.

Practise

Practise 1

Practise 2

Practise 3

TIP Remember, look up each word in your dictionary to learn its meaning!

Need extra practise?
Printable blank practise sheet available from: www.lifelongeducation.com.au/spelling_practise_sheet
(also available on page 167)

SET 6

Date: ....

Word List

passage	**publication**	**ultimate**	**territory**	**therapy**
downtown	**negotiate**	**excellent**	**succeed**	**scientific**
political	**instructor**	**protein**	**magnetic**	**entrance**

INSTRUCTIONS: Review the word list above and then cover. Have someone read out each word while you write them in the spaces below. Review any misspelt words 3 times.

LOOK. SAY. COVER. WRITE. CHECK.

Practise

Practise 1

Practise 2

Practise 3

TIP Remember, look up each word in your dictionary to learn its meaning!

Need extra practise?
Printable blank practise sheet available from: www.lifelongeducation.com.au/spelling_practise_sheet
(also available on page 167)

SET 7

Date: ....

Word List

strategic	**orientation**	**motivate**	**spectacular**	**theological**
violation	**coalition**	**communicate**	**entirely**	**signature**
difficult	**persist**	**agriculture**	**comprehensive**	**photograph**

INSTRUCTIONS: Review the word list above and then cover. Have someone read out each word while you write them in the spaces below. Review any misspelt words 3 times.

LOOK. SAY. COVER. WRITE. CHECK.

Practise

Practise 1

Practise 2

Practise 3

TIP Remember, look up each word in your dictionary to learn its meaning!

Need extra practise?
Printable blank practise sheet available from: www.lifelongeducation.com.au/spelling_practise_sheet
(also available on page 167)

SET 8

Date: ....

Word List

inspector	**overwhelm**	**herself**	**disturbing**	**improved**
biology	**partial**	**estimated**	**manager**	**casualty**
gradually	**surveillance**	**convict**	**counter**	**including**

INSTRUCTIONS: Review the word list above and then cover. Have someone read out each word while you write them in the spaces below. Review any misspelt words 3 times.

LOOK. SAY. COVER. WRITE. CHECK.

Practise

Practise 1

Practise 2

Practise 3

TIP Remember, look up each word in your dictionary to learn its meaning!

Need extra practise?
Printable blank practise sheet available from: www.lifelongeducation.com.au/spelling_practise_sheet
(also available on page 167)

SET 9

Date: ....

Word List

southwest	**shareholder**	**reserve**	**longtime**	**amazing**
excited	**demonstration**	**suggest**	**uncertain**	**tablespoon**
lifetime	**contend**	**material**	**remarkable**	**pregnancy**

INSTRUCTIONS: Review the word list above and then cover. Have someone read out each word while you write them in the spaces below. Review any misspelt words 3 times.

LOOK. SAY. COVER. WRITE. CHECK.

Practise

Practise 1

Practise 2

Practise 3

TIP Remember, look up each word in your dictionary to learn its meaning!

Need extra practise?
Printable blank practise sheet available from: www.lifelongeducation.com.au/spelling_practise_sheet
(also available on page 167)

SET 10

Date: ....

Word List

contemplate	**storage**	**desperate**	**anniversary**	**residence**
acceptable	**compare**	**formation**	**teenager**	**regional**
another	**monument**	**portray**	**plaintiff**	**acknowledge**

INSTRUCTIONS: Review the word list above and then cover. Have someone read out each word while you write them in the spaces below. Review any misspelt words 3 times.

LOOK. SAY. COVER. WRITE. CHECK.

Practise

Practise 1

Practise 2

Practise 3

TIP Remember, look up each word in your dictionary to learn its meaning!

Need extra practise?
Printable blank practise sheet available from: www.lifelongeducation.com.au/spelling_practise_sheet
(also available on page 167)

SET 11

Date: ....

Word List

starter	**judicial**	**ourselves**	**regulatory**	**penalty**
execution	**departure**	**crystal**	**diamond**	**warning**
consider	**transaction**	**problem**	**dangerous**	**development**

INSTRUCTIONS: Review the word list above and then cover. Have someone read out each word while you write them in the spaces below. Review any misspelt words 3 times.

LOOK. SAY. COVER. WRITE. CHECK.

Practise

Practise 1

Practise 2

Practise 3

TIP Remember, look up each word in your dictionary to learn its meaning!

Need extra practise?
Printable blank practise sheet available from: www.lifelongeducation.com.au/spelling_practise_sheet
(also available on page 167)

SET 12

Date: ....

Word List

invitation	**innocent**	**disorder**	**Supreme**	**slavery**
planner	**originally**	**deposit**	**elderly**	**handful**
architect	**dessert**	**managing**	**relation**	**prosecutor**

INSTRUCTIONS: Review the word list above and then cover. Have someone read out each word while you write them in the spaces below. Review any misspelt words 3 times.

LOOK. SAY. COVER. WRITE. CHECK.

Practise

Practise 1

Practise 2

Practise 3

TIP Remember, look up each word in your dictionary to learn its meaning!

Need extra practise?
Printable blank practise sheet available from: www.lifelongeducation.com.au/spelling_practise_sheet
(also available on page 167)

SET 13

Date: ....

Word List

restore	**documentary**	**significance**	**ecosystem**	**dispute**
insurance	**historical**	**respondent**	**fashion**	**pension**
textbook	**uncertainty**	**conduct**	**license**	**coverage**

INSTRUCTIONS: Review the word list above and then cover. Have someone read out each word while you write them in the spaces below. Review any misspelt words 3 times.

LOOK. SAY. COVER. WRITE. CHECK.

Practise

Practise 1

Practise 2

Practise 3

TIP Remember, look up each word in your dictionary to learn its meaning!

Need extra practise?
Printable blank practise sheet available from: www.lifelongeducation.com.au/spelling_practise_sheet
(also available on page 167)

SET 14

Date: ....

Word List

include	**enthusiasm**	**unlikely**	**despite**	**extended**
approximately	**previously**	**package**	**initially**	**stereotype**
telescope	**temperature**	**disaster**	**appropriate**	**wealthy**

INSTRUCTIONS: Review the word list above and then cover. Have someone read out each word while you write them in the spaces below. Review any misspelt words 3 times.

LOOK. SAY. COVER. WRITE. CHECK.

Practise

Practise 1

Practise 2

Practise 3

TIP Remember, look up each word in your dictionary to learn its meaning!

Need extra practise?
Printable blank practise sheet available from: www.lifelongeducation.com.au/spelling_practise_sheet
(also available on page 167)

SET 15

Date: ....

Word List

faculty	**shuttle**	**victory**	**profound**	**produce**
nutrient	**significantly**	**explosion**	**endorse**	**chronic**
discipline	**implementation**	**proportion**	**revolutionary**	**recipient**

INSTRUCTIONS: Review the word list above and then cover. Have someone read out each word while you write them in the spaces below. Review any misspelt words 3 times.

LOOK. SAY. COVER. WRITE. CHECK.

Practise

Practise 1

Practise 2

Practise 3

TIP Remember, look up each word in your dictionary to learn its meaning!

Need extra practise?
Printable blank practise sheet available from: www.lifelongeducation.com.au/spelling_practise_sheet
(also available on page 167)

SET 16

Date: ....

Word List

subject	**vaccine**	**consistent**	**habitat**	**leading**
boundary	**balance**	**helpful**	**laughter**	**associated**
competitor	**diverse**	**shortly**	**short-term**	**perceive**

INSTRUCTIONS: Review the word list above and then cover. Have someone read out each word while you write them in the spaces below. Review any misspelt words 3 times.

LOOK. SAY. COVER. WRITE. CHECK.

Practise

Practise 1

Practise 2

Practise 3

TIP Remember, look up each word in your dictionary to learn its meaning!

Need extra practise?
Printable blank practise sheet available from: www.lifelongeducation.com.au/spelling_practise_sheet
(also available on page 167)

SET 17

Date: ....

Word List

besides	**informal**	**instead**	**representative**	**lightly**
confess	**ordinary**	**various**	**protective**	**fragment**
awareness	**Italian**	**squeeze**	**environment**	**generation**

INSTRUCTIONS: Review the word list above and then cover. Have someone read out each word while you write them in the spaces below. Review any misspelt words 3 times.

LOOK. SAY. COVER. WRITE. CHECK.

Practise

Practise 1

Practise 2

Practise 3

TIP Remember, look up each word in your dictionary to learn its meaning!

Need extra practise?
Printable blank practise sheet available from: www.lifelongeducation.com.au/spelling_practise_sheet
(also available on page 167)

SET 18

Date: ....

Word List

midnight	**screening**	**mathematics**	**consist**	**characterise**
upstairs	**require**	**creation**	**independent**	**highway**
interfere	**radical**	**old-fashioned**	**prevention**	**release**

INSTRUCTIONS: Review the word list above and then cover. Have someone read out each word while you write them in the spaces below. Review any misspelt words 3 times.

LOOK. SAY. COVER. WRITE. CHECK.

Practise

Practise 1

Practise 2

Practise 3

TIP Remember, look up each word in your dictionary to learn its meaning!

Need extra practise?
Printable blank practise sheet available from: www.lifelongeducation.com.au/spelling_practise_sheet
(also available on page 167)

SET 19

Date: ....

Word List

traffic	**illustrate**	**distant**	**effectively**	**popularity**
teacher	**selection**	**recently**	**decision**	**catalogue**
minister	**Japanese**	**consultant**	**engagement**	**survivor**

INSTRUCTIONS: Review the word list above and then cover. Have someone read out each word while you write them in the spaces below. Review any misspelt words 3 times.

LOOK. SAY. COVER. WRITE. CHECK.

Practise

Practise 1

Practise 2

Practise 3

TIP Remember, look up each word in your dictionary to learn its meaning!

Need extra practise?
Printable blank practise sheet available from: www.lifelongeducation.com.au/spelling_practise_sheet
(also available on page 167)

SET 20

Date: ....

Word List

vacation	**productivity**	**following**	**specialty**	**possibility**
correlation	**homeless**	**healthcare**	**musician**	**identical**
feather	**recession**	**reflect**	**scramble**	**accomplish**

INSTRUCTIONS: Review the word list above and then cover. Have someone read out each word while you write them in the spaces below. Review any misspelt words 3 times.

LOOK. SAY. COVER. WRITE. CHECK.

Practise

Practise 1

Practise 2

Practise 3

TIP Remember, look up each word in your dictionary to learn its meaning!

Need extra practise?
Printable blank practise sheet available from: www.lifelongeducation.com.au/spelling_practise_sheet
(also available on page 167)

SET 21

Date: ....

Word List

lawsuit	**radiation**	**handsome**	**conservation**	**touchdown**
promise	**training**	**purpose**	**prospect**	**secular**
prevail	**participate**	**suspicion**	**peasant**	**assignment**

INSTRUCTIONS: Review the word list above and then cover. Have someone read out each word while you write them in the spaces below. Review any misspelt words 3 times.

LOOK. SAY. COVER. WRITE. CHECK.

Practise

Practise 1

Practise 2

Practise 3

TIP Remember, look up each word in your dictionary to learn its meaning!

Need extra practise?
Printable blank practise sheet available from: www.lifelongeducation.com.au/spelling_practise_sheet
(also available on page 167)

SET 22

Date: ....

Word List

desperately	**announce**	**prediction**	**passenger**	**employment**
example	**conclusion**	**highlight**	**anybody**	**unfortunately**
moreover	**operator**	**consideration**	**columnist**	**economy**

INSTRUCTIONS: Review the word list above and then cover. Have someone read out each word while you write them in the spaces below. Review any misspelt words 3 times.

LOOK. SAY. COVER. WRITE. CHECK.

Practise

Practise 1

Practise 2

Practise 3

TIP Remember, look up each word in your dictionary to learn its meaning!

Need extra practise?
Printable blank practise sheet available from: www.lifelongeducation.com.au/spelling_practise_sheet
(also available on page 167)

SET 23

Date: ....

Word List

television	**servant**	**transfer**	**shelter**	**isolation**
connection	**justice**	**sacrifice**	**verdict**	**diminish**
concerning	**officially**	**veteran**	**personal**	**sculpture**

INSTRUCTIONS: Review the word list above and then cover. Have someone read out each word while you write them in the spaces below. Review any misspelt words 3 times.

LOOK. SAY. COVER. WRITE. CHECK.

Practise

Practise 1

Practise 2

Practise 3

TIP Remember, look up each word in your dictionary to learn its meaning!

Need extra practise?
Printable blank practise sheet available from: www.lifelongeducation.com.au/spelling_practise_sheet
(also available on page 167)

SET 24

Date: ....

Word List

cluster	**medical**	**provider**	**defendant**	**portion**
naturally	**landmark**	**disclose**	**national**	**guideline**
Christianity	**foundation**	**prevent**	**sympathy**	**relevant**

INSTRUCTIONS: Review the word list above and then cover. Have someone read out each word while you write them in the spaces below. Review any misspelt words 3 times.

LOOK. SAY. COVER. WRITE. CHECK.

Practise

Practise 1

Practise 2

Practise 3

TIP Remember, look up each word in your dictionary to learn its meaning!

Need extra practise?
Printable blank practise sheet available from: www.lifelongeducation.com.au/spelling_practise_sheet
(also available on page 167)

SET 25

Date: ....

Word List

newspaper	**attorney**	**accommodate**	**tournament**	**reaction**
frequent	**married**	**notebook**	**exploration**	**critical**
revenue	**committee**	**privacy**	**teenage**	**starting**

INSTRUCTIONS: Review the word list above and then cover. Have someone read out each word while you write them in the spaces below. Review any misspelt words 3 times.

LOOK. SAY. COVER. WRITE. CHECK.

Practise

Practise 1

Practise 2

Practise 3

TIP Remember, look up each word in your dictionary to learn its meaning!

Need extra practise?
Printable blank practise sheet available from: www.lifelongeducation.com.au/spelling_practise_sheet
(also available on page 167)

SET 26

Date: ....

Word List

one-third	**related**	**evening**	**controversy**	**painful**
respect	**prescription**	**impossible**	**reflection**	**product**
abstract	**exercise**	**management**	**advance**	**bankruptcy**

INSTRUCTIONS: Review the word list above and then cover. Have someone read out each word while you write them in the spaces below. Review any misspelt words 3 times.

LOOK. SAY. COVER. WRITE. CHECK.

Practise

Practise 1

Practise 2

Practise 3

TIP Remember, look up each word in your dictionary to learn its meaning!

Need extra practise?
Printable blank practise sheet available from: www.lifelongeducation.com.au/spelling_practise_sheet
(also available on page 167)

SET 27

Date: ....

Word List

elsewhere	**individual**	**similarly**	**solution**	**emotional**
virtually	**creature**	**celebration**	**somewhere**	**confirm**
sophisticated	**natural**	**controversial**	**apologise**	**capability**

INSTRUCTIONS: Review the word list above and then cover. Have someone read out each word while you write them in the spaces below. Review any misspelt words 3 times.

LOOK. SAY. COVER. WRITE. CHECK.

Practise

Practise 1

Practise 2

Practise 3

TIP Remember, look up each word in your dictionary to learn its meaning!

Need extra practise?
Printable blank practise sheet available from: www.lifelongeducation.com.au/spelling_practise_sheet
(also available on page 167)

SET 28

Date: ....

Word List

creative	**literally**	**T-shirt**	**terrorism**	**president**
practical	**disease**	**swimming**	**increasingly**	**laundry**
component	**tolerate**	**satellite**	**translation**	**implication**

INSTRUCTIONS: Review the word list above and then cover. Have someone read out each word while you write them in the spaces below. Review any misspelt words 3 times.

LOOK. SAY. COVER. WRITE. CHECK.

Practise

Practise 1

Practise 2

Practise 3

TIP Remember, look up each word in your dictionary to learn its meaning!

Need extra practise?
Printable blank practise sheet available from: www.lifelongeducation.com.au/spelling_practise_sheet
(also available on page 167)

SET 29

Date: ....

Word List

improve	**doorway**	**biological**	**dictate**	**suburban**
explanation	**complete**	**baseball**	**emergency**	**opening**
high-tech	**evolution**	**fatigue**	**emerging**	**surprisingly**

INSTRUCTIONS: Review the word list above and then cover. Have someone read out each word while you write them in the spaces below. Review any misspelt words 3 times.

LOOK. SAY. COVER. WRITE. CHECK.

Practise

Practise 1

Practise 2

Practise 3

TIP Remember, look up each word in your dictionary to learn its meaning!

Need extra practise?
Printable blank practise sheet available from: www.lifelongeducation.com.au/spelling_practise_sheet
(also available on page 167)

SET 30

Date: ....

Word List

symbolic	**installation**	**transport**	**integrated**	**superior**
confusion	**expertise**	**because**	**delivery**	**electric**
realistic	**bathroom**	**emotion**	**dignity**	**unexpected**

INSTRUCTIONS: Review the word list above and then cover. Have someone read out each word while you write them in the spaces below. Review any misspelt words 3 times.

LOOK. SAY. COVER. WRITE. CHECK.

Practise

Practise 1

Practise 2

Practise 3

TIP Remember, look up each word in your dictionary to learn its meaning!

Need extra practise?
Printable blank practise sheet available from: www.lifelongeducation.com.au/spelling_practise_sheet
(also available on page 167)

SET 31

Date: ....

Word List

opposed	**sharply**	**grandfather**	**regulate**	**accountability**
circumstance	**commodity**	**village**	**frequently**	**civilization**
curious	**athletic**	**possibly**	**reservation**	**tragedy**

INSTRUCTIONS: Review the word list above and then cover. Have someone read out each word while you write them in the spaces below. Review any misspelt words 3 times.

LOOK. SAY. COVER. WRITE. CHECK.

Practise

Practise 1

Practise 2

Practise 3

TIP Remember, look up each word in your dictionary to learn its meaning!

Need extra practise?
Printable blank practise sheet available from: www.lifelongeducation.com.au/spelling_practise_sheet
(also available on page 167)

SET 32

Date: ....

Word List

equality	**championship**	**institution**	**apparent**	**privately**
classic	**analysis**	**chamber**	**neighbor**	**accuracy**
reminder	**full-time**	**current**	**closely**	**friendship**

INSTRUCTIONS: Review the word list above and then cover. Have someone read out each word while you write them in the spaces below. Review any misspelt words 3 times.

LOOK. SAY. COVER. WRITE. CHECK.

Practise

Practise 1

Practise 2

Practise 3

TIP Remember, look up each word in your dictionary to learn its meaning!

Need extra practise?
Printable blank practise sheet available from: www.lifelongeducation.com.au/spelling_practise_sheet
(also available on page 167)

SET 33

Date: ....

Word List

volunteer	**everything**	**venture**	**deliver**	**particle**
basement	**universal**	**finally**	**compose**	**sometime**
original	**conclude**	**criticism**	**sovereignty**	**agreement**

INSTRUCTIONS: Review the word list above and then cover. Have someone read out each word while you write them in the spaces below. Review any misspelt words 3 times.

LOOK. SAY. COVER. WRITE. CHECK.

Practise

Practise 1

Practise 2

Practise 3

TIP Remember, look up each word in your dictionary to learn its meaning!

Need extra practise?
Printable blank practise sheet available from: www.lifelongeducation.com.au/spelling_practise_sheet
(also available on page 167)

SET 34

Date: ....

Word List

normally	**tradition**	**minority**	**producer**	**application**
silence	**curriculum**	**ambition**	**prepare**	**similarity**
typical	**infection**	**religion**	**division**	**eliminate**

INSTRUCTIONS: Review the word list above and then cover. Have someone read out each word while you write them in the spaces below. Review any misspelt words 3 times.

LOOK. SAY. COVER. WRITE. CHECK.

Practise

Practise 1

Practise 2

Practise 3

TIP Remember, look up each word in your dictionary to learn its meaning!

Need extra practise?
Printable blank practise sheet available from: www.lifelongeducation.com.au/spelling_practise_sheet
(also available on page 167)

SET 35

Date: ....

Word List

organise	**breathing**	**slightly**	**Australian**	**compelling**
college	**instrument**	**phenomenon**	**required**	**whether**
impressive	**international**	**observer**	**potentially**	**announcement**

INSTRUCTIONS: Review the word list above and then cover. Have someone read out each word while you write them in the spaces below. Review any misspelt words 3 times.

LOOK. SAY. COVER. WRITE. CHECK.

Practise

Practise 1

Practise 2

Practise 3

TIP Remember, look up each word in your dictionary to learn its meaning!

Need extra practise?
Printable blank practise sheet available from: www.lifelongeducation.com.au/spelling_practise_sheet
(also available on page 167)

SET 36

Date: ....

Word List

illness	**complicated**	**practice**	**physician**	**transmit**
decorate	**photographer**	**curiosity**	**membership**	**inspire**
costume	**substantially**	**threaten**	**necessity**	**vulnerable**

INSTRUCTIONS: Review the word list above and then cover. Have someone read out each word while you write them in the spaces below. Review any misspelt words 3 times.

LOOK. SAY. COVER. WRITE. CHECK.

Practise

Practise 1

Practise 2

Practise 3

TIP Remember, look up each word in your dictionary to learn its meaning!

Need extra practise?
Printable blank practise sheet available from: www.lifelongeducation.com.au/spelling_practise_sheet
(also available on page 167)

SET 37

Date: ....

Word List

settlement	**proposed**	**specify**	**arrangement**	**insight**
extremely	**workplace**	**promising**	**undergo**	**performer**
cooking	**well-being**	**display**	**instance**	**ancestor**

INSTRUCTIONS: Review the word list above and then cover. Have someone read out each word while you write them in the spaces below. Review any misspelt words 3 times.

LOOK. SAY. COVER. WRITE. CHECK.

Practise

Practise 1

Practise 2

Practise 3

TIP Remember, look up each word in your dictionary to learn its meaning!

Need extra practise?
Printable blank practise sheet available from: www.lifelongeducation.com.au/spelling_practise_sheet
(also available on page 167)

SET 38

Date: ....

Word List

comparable	**request**	**suspect**	**teaching**	**reception**
western	**formula**	**composition**	**tobacco**	**instant**
clearly	**external**	**birthday**	**operating**	**nothing**

INSTRUCTIONS: Review the word list above and then cover. Have someone read out each word while you write them in the spaces below. Review any misspelt words 3 times.

LOOK. SAY. COVER. WRITE. CHECK.

Practise

Practise 1

Practise 2

Practise 3

TIP Remember, look up each word in your dictionary to learn its meaning!

Need extra practise?
Printable blank practise sheet available from: www.lifelongeducation.com.au/spelling_practise_sheet
(also available on page 167)

SET 39

Date: ....

Word List

suitable	**finance**	**attention**	**inspiration**	**tomorrow**
understand	**argument**	**partner**	**collection**	**leadership**
resemble	**response**	**electronics**	**publisher**	**drawing**

INSTRUCTIONS: Review the word list above and then cover. Have someone read out each word while you write them in the spaces below. Review any misspelt words 3 times.

LOOK. SAY. COVER. WRITE. CHECK.

Practise

Practise 1

Practise 2

Practise 3

TIP Remember, look up each word in your dictionary to learn its meaning!

Need extra practise?
Printable blank practise sheet available from: www.lifelongeducation.com.au/spelling_practise_sheet
(also available on page 167)

SET 40

Date: ....

Word List

interesting	**demographic**	**contributor**	**intense**	**acceptance**
digital	**liability**	**pursuit**	**yourself**	**rhetoric**
democratic	**concentration**	**therapist**	**convinced**	**culture**

INSTRUCTIONS: Review the word list above and then cover. Have someone read out each word while you write them in the spaces below. Review any misspelt words 3 times.

LOOK. SAY. COVER. WRITE. CHECK.

Practise

Practise 1

Practise 2

Practise 3

TIP Remember, look up each word in your dictionary to learn its meaning!

Need extra practise?
Printable blank practise sheet available from: www.lifelongeducation.com.au/spelling_practise_sheet
(also available on page 167)

SET 41

Date: ....

Word List

effective	**potential**	**version**	**condition**	**medicine**
examine	**incredibly**	**jurisdiction**	**demonstrate**	**innovation**
expression	**subsidy**	**standing**	**objective**	**ridiculous**

INSTRUCTIONS: Review the word list above and then cover. Have someone read out each word while you write them in the spaces below. Review any misspelt words 3 times.

LOOK. SAY. COVER. WRITE. CHECK.

Practise

Practise 1

Practise 2

Practise 3

TIP Remember, look up each word in your dictionary to learn its meaning!

Need extra practise?
Printable blank practise sheet available from: www.lifelongeducation.com.au/spelling_practise_sheet
(also available on page 167)

SET 42

Date: ....

Word List

railroad	**finding**	**excitement**	**biography**	**express**
scandal	**hormone**	**continent**	**behavior**	**classroom**
alleged	**partially**	**liberty**	**certain**	**isolated**

INSTRUCTIONS: Review the word list above and then cover. Have someone read out each word while you write them in the spaces below. Review any misspelt words 3 times.

LOOK. SAY. COVER. WRITE. CHECK.

Practise

Practise 1

Practise 2

Practise 3

TIP Remember, look up each word in your dictionary to learn its meaning!

Need extra practise?
Printable blank practise sheet available from: www.lifelongeducation.com.au/spelling_practise_sheet
(also available on page 167)

SET 43

Date: ....

Word List

technology	**gravity**	**scientist**	**seriously**	**combination**
philosophical	**mechanic**	**calculation**	**sweater**	**fifteen**
killing	**speculate**	**replace**	**association**	**punishment**

INSTRUCTIONS: Review the word list above and then cover. Have someone read out each word while you write them in the spaces below. Review any misspelt words 3 times.

LOOK. SAY. COVER. WRITE. CHECK.

Practise

Practise 1

Practise 2

Practise 3

TIP Remember, look up each word in your dictionary to learn its meaning!

Need extra practise?
Printable blank practise sheet available from: www.lifelongeducation.com.au/spelling_practise_sheet
(also available on page 167)

SET 44

Date: ....

Word List

brilliant	**research**	**offender**	**surprising**	**cooperation**
unemployment	**stretch**	**frontier**	**carefully**	**limited**
civilian	**overall**	**discussion**	**eventually**	**artificial**

INSTRUCTIONS: Review the word list above and then cover. Have someone read out each word while you write them in the spaces below. Review any misspelt words 3 times.

LOOK. SAY. COVER. WRITE. CHECK.

Practise

Practise 1

Practise 2

Practise 3

TIP Remember, look up each word in your dictionary to learn its meaning!

Need extra practise?
Printable blank practise sheet available from: www.lifelongeducation.com.au/spelling_practise_sheet
(also available on page 167)

SET 45

Date: ....

Word List

practically	**generally**	**premise**	**testimony**	**stumble**
provoke	**convenience**	**undertake**	**policeman**	**clinical**
counselor	**resolve**	**diagnose**	**program**	**corridor**

INSTRUCTIONS: Review the word list above and then cover. Have someone read out each word while you write them in the spaces below. Review any misspelt words 3 times.

LOOK. SAY. COVER. WRITE. CHECK.

Practise

Practise 1

Practise 2

Practise 3

TIP Remember, look up each word in your dictionary to learn its meaning!

Need extra practise?
Printable blank practise sheet available from: www.lifelongeducation.com.au/spelling_practise_sheet
(also available on page 167)

SET 46

Date: ....

Word List

diplomat	**election**	**airport**	**emission**	**reinforce**
combine	**represent**	**percentage**	**respond**	**personally**
horizon	**equipment**	**observe**	**process**	**ownership**

INSTRUCTIONS: Review the word list above and then cover. Have someone read out each word while you write them in the spaces below. Review any misspelt words 3 times.

LOOK. SAY. COVER. WRITE. CHECK.

Practise

Practise 1

Practise 2

Practise 3

TIP Remember, look up each word in your dictionary to learn its meaning!

Need extra practise?
Printable blank practise sheet available from: www.lifelongeducation.com.au/spelling_practise_sheet
(also available on page 167)

SET 47

Date: ....

Word List

predict	**professor**	**negative**	**combined**	**reasonable**
eyebrow	**accessible**	**mortality**	**journalist**	**manipulate**
strange	**translate**	**declare**	**psychological**	**charity**

INSTRUCTIONS: Review the word list above and then cover. Have someone read out each word while you write them in the spaces below. Review any misspelt words 3 times.

LOOK. SAY. COVER. WRITE. CHECK.

Practise

Practise 1

Practise 2

Practise 3

TIP Remember, look up each word in your dictionary to learn its meaning!

Need extra practise?
Printable blank practise sheet available from: www.lifelongeducation.com.au/spelling_practise_sheet
(also available on page 167)

SET 48

Date: ....

Word List

utility	**hunting**	**driveway**	**private**	**Hispanic**
speculation	**rapidly**	**syndrome**	**parental**	**maximum**
regular	**particularly**	**northwest**	**witness**	**administrative**

INSTRUCTIONS: Review the word list above and then cover. Have someone read out each word while you write them in the spaces below. Review any misspelt words 3 times.

LOOK. SAY. COVER. WRITE. CHECK.

Practise

Practise 1

Practise 2

Practise 3

TIP Remember, look up each word in your dictionary to learn its meaning!

Need extra practise?
Printable blank practise sheet available from: www.lifelongeducation.com.au/spelling_practise_sheet
(also available on page 167)

SET 49

Date: ....

Word List

companion	**patience**	**article**	**preserve**	**activist**
chairman	**ultimately**	**competition**	**projection**	**billion**
coordinator	**planning**	**occasionally**	**continue**	**proposal**

INSTRUCTIONS: Review the word list above and then cover. Have someone read out each word while you write them in the spaces below. Review any misspelt words 3 times.

LOOK. SAY. COVER. WRITE. CHECK.

Practise

Practise 1

Practise 2

Practise 3

TIP Remember, look up each word in your dictionary to learn its meaning!

Need extra practise?
Printable blank practise sheet available from: www.lifelongeducation.com.au/spelling_practise_sheet
(also available on page 167)

SET 50

Date: ....

Word List

presentation	**significant**	**magnitude**	**exception**	**investigator**
cholesterol	**dominate**	**concentrate**	**reveal**	**well-known**
organised	**question**	**aesthetic**	**fundamental**	**fascinating**

INSTRUCTIONS: Review the word list above and then cover. Have someone read out each word while you write them in the spaces below. Review any misspelt words 3 times.

LOOK. SAY. COVER. WRITE. CHECK.

Practise

Practise 1

Practise 2

Practise 3

TIP Remember, look up each word in your dictionary to learn its meaning!

Need extra practise?
Printable blank practise sheet available from: www.lifelongeducation.com.au/spelling_practise_sheet
(also available on page 167)

SET 51

Date: ....

Word List

adoption	**portrait**	**primarily**	**lighting**	**neither**
tremendous	**correspondent**	**interview**	**depression**	**automatic**
custody	**evaluation**	**o'clock**	**trading**	**architecture**

INSTRUCTIONS: Review the word list above and then cover. Have someone read out each word while you write them in the spaces below. Review any misspelt words 3 times.

LOOK. SAY. COVER. WRITE. CHECK.

Practise

Practise 1

Practise 2

Practise 3

TIP Remember, look up each word in your dictionary to learn its meaning!

Need extra practise?
Printable blank practise sheet available from: www.lifelongeducation.com.au/spelling_practise_sheet
(also available on page 167)

SET 52

Date: ....

Word List

investigate	**destroy**	**immediate**	**readily**	**restaurant**
cognitive	**hospital**	**ingredient**	**authorise**	**attract**
happiness	**justify**	**secondary**	**collector**	**reputation**

INSTRUCTIONS: Review the word list above and then cover. Have someone read out each word while you write them in the spaces below. Review any misspelt words 3 times.

LOOK. SAY. COVER. WRITE. CHECK.

Practise

Practise 1

Practise 2

Practise 3

TIP Remember, look up each word in your dictionary to learn its meaning!

Need extra practise?
Printable blank practise sheet available from: www.lifelongeducation.com.au/spelling_practise_sheet
(also available on page 167)

SET 53

Date: ....

Word List

adjustment	**reading**	**measure**	**beginning**	**standard**
advertising	**inevitably**	**different**	**associate**	**powerful**
dedicate	**forward**	**wedding**	**talented**	**quarterback**

INSTRUCTIONS: Review the word list above and then cover. Have someone read out each word while you write them in the spaces below. Review any misspelt words 3 times.

LOOK. SAY. COVER. WRITE. CHECK.

Practise

Practise 1

Practise 2

Practise 3

TIP Remember, look up each word in your dictionary to learn its meaning!

Need extra practise?
Printable blank practise sheet available from: www.lifelongeducation.com.au/spelling_practise_sheet
(also available on page 167)

SET 54

Date: ....

Word List

interest	**compete**	**hostile**	**incredible**	**literary**
reference	**existing**	**hesitate**	**purchase**	**written**
nervous	**company**	**closest**	**construct**	**ambitious**

INSTRUCTIONS: Review the word list above and then cover. Have someone read out each word while you write them in the spaces below. Review any misspelt words 3 times.

LOOK. SAY. COVER. WRITE. CHECK.

Practise

Practise 1

Practise 2

Practise 3

TIP Remember, look up each word in your dictionary to learn its meaning!

Need extra practise?
Printable blank practise sheet available from: www.lifelongeducation.com.au/spelling_practise_sheet
(also available on page 167)

SET 55

Date: ....

Word List

specialist	**exhaust**	**terrain**	**pitcher**	**requirement**
celebrity	**anxious**	**metropolitan**	**install**	**sufficient**
continued	**resistance**	**relationship**	**halfway**	**mission**

INSTRUCTIONS: Review the word list above and then cover. Have someone read out each word while you write them in the spaces below. Review any misspelt words 3 times.

LOOK. SAY. COVER. WRITE. CHECK.

Practise

Practise 1

Practise 2

Practise 3

TIP Remember, look up each word in your dictionary to learn its meaning!

Need extra practise?
Printable blank practise sheet available from: www.lifelongeducation.com.au/spelling_practise_sheet
(also available on page 167)

SET 56

Date: ....

Word List

formerly	**administration**	**influence**	**inevitable**	**hundred**
progressive	**advantage**	**outsider**	**ecological**	**southern**
entertainment	**facilitate**	**investor**	**butterfly**	**instructional**

INSTRUCTIONS: Review the word list above and then cover. Have someone read out each word while you write them in the spaces below. Review any misspelt words 3 times.

LOOK. SAY. COVER. WRITE. CHECK.

Practise

Practise 1

Practise 2

Practise 3

TIP Remember, look up each word in your dictionary to learn its meaning!

Need extra practise?
Printable blank practise sheet available from: www.lifelongeducation.com.au/spelling_practise_sheet
(also available on page 167)

SET 57

Date: ....

Word List

shortage	**ongoing**	**partnership**	**achieve**	**nevertheless**
favourable	**European**	**disappear**	**describe**	**distinction**
adventure	**otherwise**	**clothes**	**homework**	**hypothesis**

INSTRUCTIONS: Review the word list above and then cover. Have someone read out each word while you write them in the spaces below. Review any misspelt words 3 times.

LOOK. SAY. COVER. WRITE. CHECK.

Practise

Practise 1

Practise 2

Practise 3

TIP Remember, look up each word in your dictionary to learn its meaning!

Need extra practise?
Printable blank practise sheet available from: www.lifelongeducation.com.au/spelling_practise_sheet
(also available on page 167)

SET 58

Date: ....

Word List

suspicious	**background**	**survival**	**crucial**	**distance**
unknown	**general**	**detective**	**considerably**	**chemical**
vitamin	**basically**	**confidence**	**sustainable**	**distract**

INSTRUCTIONS: Review the word list above and then cover. Have someone read out each word while you write them in the spaces below. Review any misspelt words 3 times.

LOOK. SAY. COVER. WRITE. CHECK.

Practise

Practise 1

Practise 2

Practise 3

TIP Remember, look up each word in your dictionary to learn its meaning!

Need extra practise?
Printable blank practise sheet available from: www.lifelongeducation.com.au/spelling_practise_sheet
(also available on page 167)

SET 59

Date: ....

Word List

carbohydrate	**Russian**	**tropical**	**history**	**factory**
freshman	**minimal**	**without**	**tension**	**straighten**
emotionally	**throughout**	**yesterday**	**observation**	**afternoon**

INSTRUCTIONS: Review the word list above and then cover. Have someone read out each word while you write them in the spaces below. Review any misspelt words 3 times.

LOOK. SAY. COVER. WRITE. CHECK.

Practise

Practise 1

Practise 2

Practise 3

TIP Remember, look up each word in your dictionary to learn its meaning!

Need extra practise?
Printable blank practise sheet available from: www.lifelongeducation.com.au/spelling_practise_sheet
(also available on page 167)

SET 60

Date: ....

Word List

refrigerator	**shallow**	**majority**	**something**	**quietly**
involvement	**feature**	**heritage**	**constitutional**	**meanwhile**
substance	**threshold**	**monthly**	**battery**	**mountain**

INSTRUCTIONS: Review the word list above and then cover. Have someone read out each word while you write them in the spaces below. Review any misspelt words 3 times.

LOOK. SAY. COVER. WRITE. CHECK.

Practise

Practise 1

Practise 2

Practise 3

TIP Remember, look up each word in your dictionary to learn its meaning!

Need extra practise?
Printable blank practise sheet available from: www.lifelongeducation.com.au/spelling_practise_sheet
(also available on page 167)

SET 61

Date: ....

Word List

security	**assault**	**artistic**	**deadline**	**progress**
citizen	**champion**	**chemistry**	**fiction**	**balanced**
distinct	**allegation**	**warehouse**	**ironically**	**property**

INSTRUCTIONS: Review the word list above and then cover. Have someone read out each word while you write them in the spaces below. Review any misspelt words 3 times.

LOOK. SAY. COVER. WRITE. CHECK.

Practise

Practise 1

Practise 2

Practise 3

TIP Remember, look up each word in your dictionary to learn its meaning!

Need extra practise?
Printable blank practise sheet available from: www.lifelongeducation.com.au/spelling_practise_sheet
(also available on page 167)

SET 62

Date: ....

Word List

account	**control**	**wherever**	**liberal**	**elegant**
presumably	**expedition**	**hearing**	**computer**	**contribution**
proceed	**foreigner**	**destination**	**initiate**	**emphasis**

INSTRUCTIONS: Review the word list above and then cover. Have someone read out each word while you write them in the spaces below. Review any misspelt words 3 times.

LOOK. SAY. COVER. WRITE. CHECK.

Practise

Practise 1

Practise 2

Practise 3

TIP Remember, look up each word in your dictionary to learn its meaning!

Need extra practise?
Printable blank practise sheet available from: www.lifelongeducation.com.au/spelling_practise_sheet
(also available on page 167)

SET 63

Date: ....

Word List

explicit	**information**	**broadcast**	**headquarters**	**against**
institutional	**concept**	**rolling**	**colorful**	**distribution**
northern	**concede**	**someone**	**removal**	**exactly**

INSTRUCTIONS: Review the word list above and then cover. Have someone read out each word while you write them in the spaces below. Review any misspelt words 3 times.

LOOK. SAY. COVER. WRITE. CHECK.

Practise

Practise 1

Practise 2

Practise 3

TIP Remember, look up each word in your dictionary to learn its meaning!

Need extra practise?
Printable blank practise sheet available from: www.lifelongeducation.com.au/spelling_practise_sheet
(also available on page 167)

SET 64

Date: ....

Word List

alliance	**dramatic**	**everybody**	**grandparent**	**fishing**
cartoon	**festival**	**mansion**	**difficulty**	**selected**
separate	**developer**	**writing**	**together**	**rehabilitation**

INSTRUCTIONS: Review the word list above and then cover. Have someone read out each word while you write them in the spaces below. Review any misspelt words 3 times.

LOOK. SAY. COVER. WRITE. CHECK.

Practise

Practise 1

Practise 2

Practise 3

TIP Remember, look up each word in your dictionary to learn its meaning!

Need extra practise?
Printable blank practise sheet available from: www.lifelongeducation.com.au/spelling_practise_sheet
(also available on page 167)

SET 65

Date: ....

Word List

recovery	**distribute**	**important**	**fraction**	**disappointed**
statistical	**whoever**	**technique**	**addition**	**revolution**
disagree	**picture**	**kingdom**	**banking**	**theology**

INSTRUCTIONS: Review the word list above and then cover. Have someone read out each word while you write them in the spaces below. Review any misspelt words 3 times.

LOOK. SAY. COVER. WRITE. CHECK.

Practise

Practise 1

Practise 2

Practise 3

TIP Remember, look up each word in your dictionary to learn its meaning!

Need extra practise?
Printable blank practise sheet available from: www.lifelongeducation.com.au/spelling_practise_sheet
(also available on page 167)

SET 66

Date: ....

Word List

precisely	**African**	**steadily**	**listener**	**community**
instruct	**criteria**	**promote**	**central**	**mushroom**
walking	**briefly**	**senator**	**skilled**	**pattern**

INSTRUCTIONS: Review the word list above and then cover. Have someone read out each word while you write them in the spaces below. Review any misspelt words 3 times.

LOOK. SAY. COVER. WRITE. CHECK.

Practise

Practise 1

Practise 2

Practise 3

TIP Remember, look up each word in your dictionary to learn its meaning!

Need extra practise?
Printable blank practise sheet available from: www.lifelongeducation.com.au/spelling_practise_sheet
(also available on page 167)

SET 67

Date: ....

Word List

suspend	**Palestinian**	**intervention**	**discrimination**	**provided**
several	**journey**	**inherent**	**certainly**	**immigration**
attitude	**reverse**	**organization**	**hardware**	**homeland**

INSTRUCTIONS: Review the word list above and then cover. Have someone read out each word while you write them in the spaces below. Review any misspelt words 3 times.

LOOK. SAY. COVER. WRITE. CHECK.

Practise

Practise 1

Practise 2

Practise 3

TIP Remember, look up each word in your dictionary to learn its meaning!

Need extra practise?
Printable blank practise sheet available from: www.lifelongeducation.com.au/spelling_practise_sheet
(also available on page 167)

SET 68

Date: ....

Word List

direction	**welfare**	**jewelry**	**immediately**	**frequency**
respectively	**initiative**	**largely**	**provide**	**rebate**
comment	**mystery**	**outline**	**especially**	**supporter**

INSTRUCTIONS: Review the word list above and then cover. Have someone read out each word while you write them in the spaces below. Review any misspelt words 3 times.

LOOK. SAY. COVER. WRITE. CHECK.

Practise

Practise 1

Practise 2

Practise 3

TIP Remember, look up each word in your dictionary to learn its meaning!

Need extra practise?
Printable blank practise sheet available from: www.lifelongeducation.com.au/spelling_practise_sheet
(also available on page 167)

SET 69

Date: ....

Word List

elephant	**discourage**	**isolate**	**perception**	**journal**
conception	**stranger**	**educator**	**flexible**	**inventory**
compensation	**mechanical**	**arrival**	**favourite**	**million**

INSTRUCTIONS: Review the word list above and then cover. Have someone read out each word while you write them in the spaces below. Review any misspelt words 3 times.

LOOK. SAY. COVER. WRITE. CHECK.

Practise

Practise 1

Practise 2

Practise 3

TIP Remember, look up each word in your dictionary to learn its meaning!

Need extra practise?
Printable blank practise sheet available from: www.lifelongeducation.com.au/spelling_practise_sheet
(also available on page 167)

SET 70

Date: ....

Word List

astronomer	**drinking**	**conscious**	**frustration**	**adequate**
restrict	**disturb**	**cabinet**	**classify**	**builder**
morning	**constitution**	**anything**	**tolerance**	**Mexican**

INSTRUCTIONS: Review the word list above and then cover. Have someone read out each word while you write them in the spaces below. Review any misspelt words 3 times.

LOOK. SAY. COVER. WRITE. CHECK.

Practise

Practise 1

Practise 2

Practise 3

TIP Remember, look up each word in your dictionary to learn its meaning!

Need extra practise?
Printable blank practise sheet available from: www.lifelongeducation.com.au/spelling_practise_sheet
(also available on page 167)

SET 71

Date: ....

Word List

graduate	**voluntary**	**support**	**objection**	**straight**
inspection	**variable**	**fighter**	**aggression**	**analyze**
production	**elementary**	**technical**	**conversion**	**discourse**

INSTRUCTIONS: Review the word list above and then cover. Have someone read out each word while you write them in the spaces below. Review any misspelt words 3 times.

LOOK. SAY. COVER. WRITE. CHECK.

Practise

Practise 1

Practise 2

Practise 3

TIP Remember, look up each word in your dictionary to learn its meaning!

Need extra practise?
Printable blank practise sheet available from: www.lifelongeducation.com.au/spelling_practise_sheet
(also available on page 167)

SET 72

Date: ....

Word List

attendance	**appreciate**	**supervisor**	**corruption**	**economics**
address	**precious**	**honestly**	**pioneer**	**chicken**
benefit	**careful**	**politically**	**physical**	**satisfy**

INSTRUCTIONS: Review the word list above and then cover. Have someone read out each word while you write them in the spaces below. Review any misspelt words 3 times.

LOOK. SAY. COVER. WRITE. CHECK.

Practise

Practise 1

Practise 2

Practise 3

TIP Remember, look up each word in your dictionary to learn its meaning!

Need extra practise?
Printable blank practise sheet available from: www.lifelongeducation.com.au/spelling_practise_sheet
(also available on page 167)

SET 73

Date: ....

Word List

activity	**building**	**artifact**	**interpret**	**probably**
intelligent	**genuine**	**enterprise**	**persuade**	**strengthen**
genetic	**description**	**evidence**	**opinion**	**literature**

INSTRUCTIONS: Review the word list above and then cover. Have someone read out each word while you write them in the spaces below. Review any misspelt words 3 times.

LOOK. SAY. COVER. WRITE. CHECK.

Practise

Practise 1

Practise 2

Practise 3

TIP Remember, look up each word in your dictionary to learn its meaning!

Need extra practise?
Printable blank practise sheet available from: www.lifelongeducation.com.au/spelling_practise_sheet
(also available on page 167)

SET 74

Date: ....

Word List

admission	**themselves**	**attribute**	**interaction**	**positive**
extensive	**professional**	**acquire**	**terrible**	**visitor**
revelation	**expected**	**passing**	**uniform**	**Republican**

INSTRUCTIONS: Review the word list above and then cover. Have someone read out each word while you write them in the spaces below. Review any misspelt words 3 times.

LOOK. SAY. COVER. WRITE. CHECK.

Practise

Practise 1

Practise 2

Practise 3

TIP Remember, look up each word in your dictionary to learn its meaning!

Need extra practise?
Printable blank practise sheet available from: www.lifelongeducation.com.au/spelling_practise_sheet
(also available on page 167)

SET 75

Date: ....

Word List

classical	**assemble**	**maintenance**	**defensive**	**Olympics**
serving	**striking**	**flexibility**	**abandon**	**student**
routinely	**mechanism**	**investment**	**developmental**	**imagine**

INSTRUCTIONS: Review the word list above and then cover. Have someone read out each word while you write them in the spaces below. Review any misspelt words 3 times.

LOOK. SAY. COVER. WRITE. CHECK.

Practise

Practise 1

Practise 2

Practise 3

TIP Remember, look up each word in your dictionary to learn its meaning!

Need extra practise?
Printable blank practise sheet available from: www.lifelongeducation.com.au/spelling_practise_sheet
(also available on page 167)

SET 76

Date: ....

Word List

neighbourhood	**obviously**	**frustrate**	**meaningful**	**legislature**
underlying	**mandate**	**foreign**	**separation**	**presidential**
arrange	**attraction**	**movement**	**scholarship**	**stimulus**

INSTRUCTIONS: Review the word list above and then cover. Have someone read out each word while you write them in the spaces below. Review any misspelt words 3 times.

LOOK. SAY. COVER. WRITE. CHECK.

Practise

Practise 1

Practise 2

Practise 3

TIP Remember, look up each word in your dictionary to learn its meaning!

Need extra practise?
Printable blank practise sheet available from: www.lifelongeducation.com.au/spelling_practise_sheet
(also available on page 167)

SET 77

Date: ....

Word List

struggle	**assessment**	**previous**	**curtain**	**analyst**
effectiveness	**prisoner**	**boyfriend**	**structure**	**comfort**
intimate	**balloon**	**backyard**	**essentially**	**self-esteem**

INSTRUCTIONS: Review the word list above and then cover. Have someone read out each word while you write them in the spaces below. Review any misspelt words 3 times.

LOOK. SAY. COVER. WRITE. CHECK.

Practise

Practise 1

Practise 2

Practise 3

TIP Remember, look up each word in your dictionary to learn its meaning!

Need extra practise?
Printable blank practise sheet available from: www.lifelongeducation.com.au/spelling_practise_sheet
(also available on page 167)

SET 78

Date: ....

Word List

mysterious	**thoroughly**	**graduation**	**guidance**	**trigger**
therefore	**accounting**	**supportive**	**disability**	**responsible**
customer	**dependent**	**worried**	**correct**	**emphasise**

INSTRUCTIONS: Review the word list above and then cover. Have someone read out each word while you write them in the spaces below. Review any misspelt words 3 times.

LOOK. SAY. COVER. WRITE. CHECK.

Practise

Practise 1

Practise 2

Practise 3

TIP Remember, look up each word in your dictionary to learn its meaning!

Need extra practise?
Printable blank practise sheet available from: www.lifelongeducation.com.au/spelling_practise_sheet
(also available on page 167)

SET 79

Date: ....

Word List

fortunately	**principal**	**profession**	**hallway**	**mortgage**
equally	**surgeon**	**confront**	**instantly**	**collective**
diabetes	**entrepreneur**	**outdoor**	**anymore**	**anonymous**

INSTRUCTIONS: Review the word list above and then cover. Have someone read out each word while you write them in the spaces below. Review any misspelt words 3 times.

LOOK. SAY. COVER. WRITE. CHECK.

Practise

Practise 1

Practise 2

Practise 3

TIP Remember, look up each word in your dictionary to learn its meaning!

Need extra practise?
Printable blank practise sheet available from: www.lifelongeducation.com.au/spelling_practise_sheet
(also available on page 167)

SET 80

Date: ....

Word List

unhappy	**complex**	**overnight**	**criticise**	**dialogue**
telephone	**exhibit**	**experiment**	**counselling**	**harmony**
manufacturing	**himself**	**loyalty**	**supplier**	**whereas**

INSTRUCTIONS: Review the word list above and then cover. Have someone read out each word while you write them in the spaces below. Review any misspelt words 3 times.

LOOK. SAY. COVER. WRITE. CHECK.

Practise

Practise 1

Practise 2

Practise 3

TIP Remember, look up each word in your dictionary to learn its meaning!

Need extra practise?
Printable blank practise sheet available from: www.lifelongeducation.com.au/spelling_practise_sheet
(also available on page 167)

SET 81

Date: ....

Word List

generous	**official**	**eligible**	**resource**	**surround**
meaning	**restriction**	**processor**	**intelligence**	**ideally**
believe	**likelihood**	**beneath**	**commitment**	**wildlife**

INSTRUCTIONS: Review the word list above and then cover. Have someone read out each word while you write them in the spaces below. Review any misspelt words 3 times.

LOOK. SAY. COVER. WRITE. CHECK.

Practise

Practise 1

Practise 2

Practise 3

TIP Remember, look up each word in your dictionary to learn its meaning!

Need extra practise?
Printable blank practise sheet available from: www.lifelongeducation.com.au/spelling_practise_sheet
(also available on page 167)

SET 82

Date: ....

Word List

disabled	**success**	**perspective**	**shopping**	**collapse**
episode	**inherit**	**governor**	**thereby**	**familiar**
completely	**someday**	**socially**	**surrounding**	**category**

INSTRUCTIONS: Review the word list above and then cover. Have someone read out each word while you write them in the spaces below. Review any misspelt words 3 times.

LOOK. SAY. COVER. WRITE. CHECK.

Practise

Practise 1

Practise 2

Practise 3

TIP Remember, look up each word in your dictionary to learn its meaning!

Need extra practise?
Printable blank practise sheet available from: www.lifelongeducation.com.au/spelling_practise_sheet
(also available on page 167)

SET 83

Date: ....

Word List

actively	**manufacturer**	**approve**	**momentum**	**withdrawal**
increasing	**perfect**	**statistics**	**undergraduate**	**illegal**
condemn	**troubled**	**preference**	**youngster**	**aircraft**

INSTRUCTIONS: Review the word list above and then cover. Have someone read out each word while you write them in the spaces below. Review any misspelt words 3 times.

LOOK. SAY. COVER. WRITE. CHECK.

Practise

Practise 1

Practise 2

Practise 3

TIP Remember, look up each word in your dictionary to learn its meaning!

Need extra practise?
Printable blank practise sheet available from: www.lifelongeducation.com.au/spelling_practise_sheet
(also available on page 167)

SET 84

Date: ....

Word List

somewhat	**privilege**	**scholar**	**outcome**	**distinctive**
optimistic	**offensive**	**reliable**	**convention**	**coordinate**
identify	**weekend**	**elevator**	**somebody**	**aggressive**

INSTRUCTIONS: Review the word list above and then cover. Have someone read out each word while you write them in the spaces below. Review any misspelt words 3 times.

LOOK. SAY. COVER. WRITE. CHECK.

Practise

Practise 1

Practise 2

Practise 3

TIP Remember, look up each word in your dictionary to learn its meaning!

Need extra practise?
Printable blank practise sheet available from: www.lifelongeducation.com.au/spelling_practise_sheet
(also available on page 167)

SET 85

Date: ....

Word List

council	**forever**	**employer**	**teammate**	**sidewalk**
seventh	**founder**	**ministry**	**absence**	**perceived**
priority	**courtroom**	**determination**	**primary**	**concrete**

INSTRUCTIONS: Review the word list above and then cover. Have someone read out each word while you write them in the spaces below. Review any misspelt words 3 times.

LOOK. SAY. COVER. WRITE. CHECK.

Practise

Practise 1

Practise 2

Practise 3

TIP Remember, look up each word in your dictionary to learn its meaning!

Need extra practise?
Printable blank practise sheet available from: www.lifelongeducation.com.au/spelling_practise_sheet
(also available on page 167)

SET 86

Date: ....

Word List

advanced	**payment**	**project**	**recommend**	**traveler**
earnings	**fighting**	**survive**	**destruction**	**trainer**
considerable	**accelerate**	**intensity**	**romance**	**assistant**

INSTRUCTIONS: Review the word list above and then cover. Have someone read out each word while you write them in the spaces below. Review any misspelt words 3 times.

LOOK. SAY. COVER. WRITE. CHECK.

Practise

Practise 1

Practise 2

Practise 3

TIP Remember, look up each word in your dictionary to learn its meaning!

Need extra practise?
Printable blank practise sheet available from: www.lifelongeducation.com.au/spelling_practise_sheet
(also available on page 167)

SET 87

Date: ....

Word List

processing	**concern**	**language**	**delight**	**monster**
simultaneously	**consumption**	**happily**	**available**	**accurately**
incentive	**ideology**	**through**	**popular**	**employee**

INSTRUCTIONS: Review the word list above and then cover. Have someone read out each word while you write them in the spaces below. Review any misspelt words 3 times.

LOOK. SAY. COVER. WRITE. CHECK.

Practise

Practise 1

Practise 2

Practise 3

TIP Remember, look up each word in your dictionary to learn its meaning!

Need extra practise?
Printable blank practise sheet available from: www.lifelongeducation.com.au/spelling_practise_sheet
(also available on page 167)

SET 88

Date: ....

Word List

integrate	**nomination**	**establish**	**perform**	**complain**
politician	**northeast**	**lawmaker**	**delicate**	**legally**
strength	**wonderful**	**twentieth**	**speaker**	**taxpayer**

INSTRUCTIONS: Review the word list above and then cover. Have someone read out each word while you write them in the spaces below. Review any misspelt words 3 times.

LOOK. SAY. COVER. WRITE. CHECK.

Practise

Practise 1

Practise 2

Practise 3

TIP Remember, look up each word in your dictionary to learn its meaning!

Need extra practise?
Printable blank practise sheet available from: www.lifelongeducation.com.au/spelling_practise_sheet
(also available on page 167)

SET 89

Date: ....

Word List

contest	**football**	**necessarily**	**engineer**	**missile**
routine	**position**	**nonprofit**	**capable**	**surprise**
dimension	**municipal**	**compliance**	**predator**	**invention**

INSTRUCTIONS: Review the word list above and then cover. Have someone read out each word while you write them in the spaces below. Review any misspelt words 3 times.

LOOK. SAY. COVER. WRITE. CHECK.

Practise

Practise 1

Practise 2

Practise 3

TIP Remember, look up each word in your dictionary to learn its meaning!

Need extra practise?
Printable blank practise sheet available from: www.lifelongeducation.com.au/spelling_practise_sheet
(also available on page 167)

SET 90

Date: ....

Word List

although	**regulator**	**carrier**	**experimental**	**enforce**
plastic	**afterward**	**diplomatic**	**academic**	**invisible**
testify	**hostage**	**fitness**	**explode**	**relieve**

INSTRUCTIONS: Review the word list above and then cover. Have someone read out each word while you write them in the spaces below. Review any misspelt words 3 times.

LOOK. SAY. COVER. WRITE. CHECK.

Practise

Practise 1

Practise 2

Practise 3

TIP Remember, look up each word in your dictionary to learn its meaning!

Need extra practise?
Printable blank practise sheet available from: www.lifelongeducation.com.au/spelling_practise_sheet
(also available on page 167)

SET 91

Date: ....

Word List

compound	**session**	**behavioral**	**annually**	**department**
teaspoon	**captain**	**lightning**	**recognise**	**crowded**
retirement	**uncover**	**economist**	**regarding**	**motivation**

INSTRUCTIONS: Review the word list above and then cover. Have someone read out each word while you write them in the spaces below. Review any misspelt words 3 times.

LOOK. SAY. COVER. WRITE. CHECK.

Practise

Practise 1

Practise 2

Practise 3

TIP Remember, look up each word in your dictionary to learn its meaning!

Need extra practise?
Printable blank practise sheet available from: www.lifelongeducation.com.au/spelling_practise_sheet
(also available on page 167)

SET 92

Date: ....

Word List

provision	**sensation**	**magazine**	**prominent**	**involve**
thought	**enforcement**	**likewise**	**gathering**	**obligation**
reporting	**reluctant**	**function**	**possible**	**advocate**

INSTRUCTIONS: Review the word list above and then cover. Have someone read out each word while you write them in the spaces below. Review any misspelt words 3 times.

LOOK. SAY. COVER. WRITE. CHECK.

Practise

Practise 1

Practise 2

Practise 3

TIP Remember, look up each word in your dictionary to learn its meaning!

Need extra practise?
Printable blank practise sheet available from: www.lifelongeducation.com.au/spelling_practise_sheet
(also available on page 167)

SET 93

Date: ....

Word List

structural	**anxiety**	**aluminum**	**average**	**fisherman**
recommendation	**continuous**	**republic**	**calendar**	**breakfast**
edition	**violence**	**platform**	**utilise**	**continuing**

INSTRUCTIONS: Review the word list above and then cover. Have someone read out each word while you write them in the spaces below. Review any misspelt words 3 times.

LOOK. SAY. COVER. WRITE. CHECK.

Practise

Practise 1

Practise 2

Practise 3

TIP Remember, look up each word in your dictionary to learn its meaning!

Need extra practise?
Printable blank practise sheet available from: www.lifelongeducation.com.au/spelling_practise_sheet
(also available on page 167)

SET 94

Date: ....

Word List

passion	**ceremony**	**harvest**	**ambassador**	**administrator**
supermarket	**complexity**	**specialise**	**hopefully**	**propose**
disappointment	**British**	**appointment**	**spokesman**	**commercial**

INSTRUCTIONS: Review the word list above and then cover. Have someone read out each word while you write them in the spaces below. Review any misspelt words 3 times.

LOOK. SAY. COVER. WRITE. CHECK.

Practise

Practise 1

Practise 2

Practise 3

TIP Remember, look up each word in your dictionary to learn its meaning!

Need extra practise?
Printable blank practise sheet available from: www.lifelongeducation.com.au/spelling_practise_sheet
(also available on page 167)

SET 95

Date: ....

Word List

spiritual	**permission**	**terrific**	**oversee**	**playoff**
citizenship	**stability**	**capital**	**characteristic**	**sprinkle**
cooperative	**apparently**	**identification**	**situation**	**productive**

INSTRUCTIONS: Review the word list above and then cover. Have someone read out each word while you write them in the spaces below. Review any misspelt words 3 times.

LOOK. SAY. COVER. WRITE. CHECK.

Practise

Practise 1

Practise 2

Practise 3

TIP Remember, look up each word in your dictionary to learn its meaning!

Need extra practise?
Printable blank practise sheet available from: www.lifelongeducation.com.au/spelling_practise_sheet
(also available on page 167)

SET 96

Date: ....

Word List

defender	**spending**	**violate**	**generate**	**alongside**
rebuild	**specifically**	**mineral**	**intention**	**undermine**
designer	**allegedly**	**virtual**	**Christmas**	**responsibility**

INSTRUCTIONS: Review the word list above and then cover. Have someone read out each word while you write them in the spaces below. Review any misspelt words 3 times.

LOOK. SAY. COVER. WRITE. CHECK.

Practise

Practise 1

Practise 2

Practise 3

TIP Remember, look up each word in your dictionary to learn its meaning!

Need extra practise?
Printable blank practise sheet available from: www.lifelongeducation.com.au/spelling_practise_sheet (also available on page 167)

SET 97

Date: ....

Word List

summary	**supposedly**	**definitely**	**consequence**	**terrorist**
developing	**romantic**	**universe**	**principle**	**retailer**
treasure	**divorce**	**candidate**	**theoretical**	**tightly**

INSTRUCTIONS: Review the word list above and then cover. Have someone read out each word while you write them in the spaces below. Review any misspelt words 3 times.

LOOK. SAY. COVER. WRITE. CHECK.

Practise

Practise 1

Practise 2

Practise 3

TIP Remember, look up each word in your dictionary to learn its meaning!

Need extra practise?
Printable blank practise sheet available from: www.lifelongeducation.com.au/spelling_practise_sheet
(also available on page 167)

SET 98

Date: ....

Word List

atmosphere	**contemporary**	**consequently**	**constantly**	**Democrat**
amendment	**already**	**poverty**	**judgment**	**concert**
pleasure	**offering**	**automatically**	**suggestion**	**strategy**

INSTRUCTIONS: Review the word list above and then cover. Have someone read out each word while you write them in the spaces below. Review any misspelt words 3 times.

LOOK. SAY. COVER. WRITE. CHECK.

Practise

Practise 1

Practise 2

Practise 3

TIP Remember, look up each word in your dictionary to learn its meaning!

Need extra practise?
Printable blank practise sheet available from: www.lifelongeducation.com.au/spelling_practise_sheet
(also available on page 167)

SET 99

Date: ....

Word List

discovery	**substantial**	**character**	**university**	**apology**
blanket	**suppose**	**education**	**sandwich**	**administer**
recruit	**stadium**	**feminist**	**qualify**	**promotion**

INSTRUCTIONS: Review the word list above and then cover. Have someone read out each word while you write them in the spaces below. Review any misspelt words 3 times.

LOOK. SAY. COVER. WRITE. CHECK.

Practise

Practise 1

Practise 2

Practise 3

TIP Remember, look up each word in your dictionary to learn its meaning!

Need extra practise?
Printable blank practise sheet available from: www.lifelongeducation.com.au/spelling_practise_sheet
(also available on page 167)

SET 100

Date: ....

Word List

construction	**cultural**	**holiday**	**totally**	**exposure**
improvement	**district**	**scatter**	**anticipate**	**household**
glimpse	**participant**	**nowhere**	**whisper**	**resolution**

INSTRUCTIONS: Review the word list above and then cover. Have someone read out each word while you write them in the spaces below. Review any misspelt words 3 times.

LOOK. SAY. COVER. WRITE. CHECK.

Practise

Practise 1

Practise 2

Practise 3

TIP Remember, look up each word in your dictionary to learn its meaning!

Need extra practise?
Printable blank practise sheet available from: www.lifelongeducation.com.au/spelling_practise_sheet
(also available on page 167)

SET 101

Date: ....

Word List

impression	**franchise**	**legislative**	**enhance**	**severely**
sponsor	**fantasy**	**practitioner**	**currency**	**airplane**
chapter	**involved**	**absolute**	**meeting**	**retired**

INSTRUCTIONS: Review the word list above and then cover. Have someone read out each word while you write them in the spaces below. Review any misspelt words 3 times.

LOOK. SAY. COVER. WRITE. CHECK.

Practise

Practise 1

Practise 2

Practise 3

TIP Remember, look up each word in your dictionary to learn its meaning!

Need extra practise?
Printable blank practise sheet available from: www.lifelongeducation.com.au/spelling_practise_sheet
(also available on page 167)

SET 102

Date: ....

Word List

forehead	**exhibition**	**earthquake**	**container**	**healthy**
instruction	**migration**	**weather**	**negotiation**	**indicate**
elaborate	**kitchen**	**pressure**	**according**	**furthermore**

INSTRUCTIONS: Review the word list above and then cover. Have someone read out each word while you write them in the spaces below. Review any misspelt words 3 times.

LOOK. SAY. COVER. WRITE. CHECK.

Practise

Practise 1

Practise 2

Practise 3

TIP Remember, look up each word in your dictionary to learn its meaning!

Need extra practise?
Printable blank practise sheet available from: www.lifelongeducation.com.au/spelling_practise_sheet
(also available on page 167)

SET 103

Date: ....

Word List

exploit	**greatly**	**tendency**	**fantastic**	**nationwide**
similar	**temporary**	**determine**	**country**	**conceive**
reality	**performance**	**communication**	**harassment**	**environmental**

INSTRUCTIONS: Review the word list above and then cover. Have someone read out each word while you write them in the spaces below. Review any misspelt words 3 times.

LOOK. SAY. COVER. WRITE. CHECK.

Practise

Practise 1

Practise 2

Practise 3

TIP Remember, look up each word in your dictionary to learn its meaning!

Need extra practise?
Printable blank practise sheet available from: www.lifelongeducation.com.au/spelling_practise_sheet
(also available on page 167)

SET 104

Date: ....

Word List

tighten	**mainstream**	**wheelchair**	**specific**	**typically**
recording	**lifestyle**	**darkness**	**proclaim**	**framework**
Israeli	**legislation**	**competitive**	**recognition**	**capture**

INSTRUCTIONS: Review the word list above and then cover. Have someone read out each word while you write them in the spaces below. Review any misspelt words 3 times.

LOOK. SAY. COVER. WRITE. CHECK.

Practise

Practise 1

Practise 2

Practise 3

TIP Remember, look up each word in your dictionary to learn its meaning!

Need extra practise?
Printable blank practise sheet available from: www.lifelongeducation.com.au/spelling_practise_sheet
(also available on page 167)

SET 105

Date: ....

Word List

auction	**counsel**	**funding**	**stomach**	**implement**
conscience	**existence**	**fragile**	**impulse**	**bicycle**
strictly	**growing**	**terribly**	**scenario**	**reduction**

INSTRUCTIONS: Review the word list above and then cover. Have someone read out each word while you write them in the spaces below. Review any misspelt words 3 times.

LOOK. SAY. COVER. WRITE. CHECK.

Practise

Practise 1

Practise 2

Practise 3

TIP Remember, look up each word in your dictionary to learn its meaning!

Need extra practise?
Printable blank practise sheet available from: www.lifelongeducation.com.au/spelling_practise_sheet
(also available on page 167)

SET 106

Date: ....

Word List

programming	**appearance**	**sentence**	**cigarette**	**expectation**
triumph	**workshop**	**nominee**	**recover**	**permanent**
extreme	**symptom**	**consensus**	**interval**	**Christian**

INSTRUCTIONS: Review the word list above and then cover. Have someone read out each word while you write them in the spaces below. Review any misspelt words 3 times.

LOOK. SAY. COVER. WRITE. CHECK.

Practise

Practise 1

Practise 2

Practise 3

TIP Remember, look up each word in your dictionary to learn its meaning!

Need extra practise?
Printable blank practise sheet available from: www.lifelongeducation.com.au/spelling_practise_sheet
(also available on page 167)

SET 107

Date: ....

Word List

engineering	**possession**	**incorporate**	**contrast**	**organic**
usually	**gallery**	**contact**	**secretary**	**conversation**
medication	**reportedly**	**explain**	**importance**	**organism**

INSTRUCTIONS: Review the word list above and then cover. Have someone read out each word while you write them in the spaces below. Review any misspelt words 3 times.

LOOK. SAY. COVER. WRITE. CHECK.

Practise

Practise 1

Practise 2

Practise 3

TIP Remember, look up each word in your dictionary to learn its meaning!

Need extra practise?
Printable blank practise sheet available from: www.lifelongeducation.com.au/spelling_practise_sheet
(also available on page 167)

SET 108

Date: ....

Word List

horrible	**testing**	**executive**	**outstanding**	**exchange**
importantly	**colleague**	**currently**	**everyday**	**obvious**
protocol	**availability**	**enormous**	**friendly**	**dissolve**

INSTRUCTIONS: Review the word list above and then cover. Have someone read out each word while you write them in the spaces below. Review any misspelt words 3 times.

LOOK. SAY. COVER. WRITE. CHECK.

Practise

Practise 1

Practise 2

Practise 3

TIP Remember, look up each word in your dictionary to learn its meaning!

Need extra practise?
Printable blank practise sheet available from: www.lifelongeducation.com.au/spelling_practise_sheet
(also available on page 167)

SET 109

Date: ....

Word List

density	**physically**	**driving**	**neighboring**	**weakness**
trailer	**actress**	**sanction**	**presidency**	**schedule**
historically	**expensive**	**interpretation**	**seemingly**	**unprecedented**

INSTRUCTIONS: Review the word list above and then cover. Have someone read out each word while you write them in the spaces below. Review any misspelt words 3 times.

LOOK. SAY. COVER. WRITE. CHECK.

Practise

Practise 1

Practise 2

Practise 3

TIP Remember, look up each word in your dictionary to learn its meaning!

Need extra practise?
Printable blank practise sheet available from: www.lifelongeducation.com.au/spelling_practise_sheet
(also available on page 167)

SET 110

Date: ....

Word List

congressional	**sensitive**	**painter**	**dominant**	**childhood**
widespread	**depressed**	**retreat**	**establishment**	**service**
transit	**inflation**	**variation**	**infrastructure**	**transmission**

INSTRUCTIONS: Review the word list above and then cover. Have someone read out each word while you write them in the spaces below. Review any misspelt words 3 times.

LOOK. SAY. COVER. WRITE. CHECK.

Practise

Practise 1

Practise 2

Practise 3

TIP Remember, look up each word in your dictionary to learn its meaning!

Need extra practise?
Printable blank practise sheet available from: www.lifelongeducation.com.au/spelling_practise_sheet
(also available on page 167)

SET 111

Date: ....

Word List

moderate	**conservative**	**doctrine**	**fortune**	**roughly**
electricity	**wilderness**	**minimum**	**basketball**	**tonight**
agricultural	**everywhere**	**leather**	**unusual**	**painting**

INSTRUCTIONS: Review the word list above and then cover. Have someone read out each word while you write them in the spaces below. Review any misspelt words 3 times.

LOOK. SAY. COVER. WRITE. CHECK.

Practise

Practise 1

Practise 2

Practise 3

TIP Remember, look up each word in your dictionary to learn its meaning!

Need extra practise?
Printable blank practise sheet available from: www.lifelongeducation.com.au/spelling_practise_sheet
(also available on page 167)

SET 112

Date: ....

Word List

merchant	**supposed**	**channel**	**capacity**	**document**
willing	**grateful**	**compromise**	**learning**	**innovative**
brother	**absolutely**	**feedback**	**defense**	**actually**

INSTRUCTIONS: Review the word list above and then cover. Have someone read out each word while you write them in the spaces below. Review any misspelt words 3 times.

LOOK. SAY. COVER. WRITE. CHECK.

Practise

Practise 1

Practise 2

Practise 3

TIP Remember, look up each word in your dictionary to learn its meaning!

Need extra practise?
Printable blank practise sheet available from: www.lifelongeducation.com.au/spelling_practise_sheet
(also available on page 167)

SET 113

Date: ....

Word List

residential	**constraint**	**subsequent**	**accomplishment**	**legislator**
satisfaction	**essential**	**financial**	**experience**	**middle-class**
headache	**personnel**	**grocery**	**educate**	**vehicle**

INSTRUCTIONS: Review the word list above and then cover. Have someone read out each word while you write them in the spaces below. Review any misspelt words 3 times.

LOOK. SAY. COVER. WRITE. CHECK.

Practise

Practise 1

Practise 2

Practise 3

TIP Remember, look up each word in your dictionary to learn its meaning!

Need extra practise?
Printable blank practise sheet available from: www.lifelongeducation.com.au/spelling_practise_sheet
(also available on page 167)

SET 114

Date: ....

Word List

increase	**politics**	**receive**	**initial**	**ancient**
preparation	**freedom**	**dismiss**	**execute**	**changing**
colonial	**population**	**texture**	**autonomy**	**directly**

INSTRUCTIONS: Review the word list above and then cover. Have someone read out each word while you write them in the spaces below. Review any misspelt words 3 times.

LOOK. SAY. COVER. WRITE. CHECK.

Practise

Practise 1

Practise 2

Practise 3

TIP Remember, look up each word in your dictionary to learn its meaning!

Need extra practise?
Printable blank practise sheet available from: www.lifelongeducation.com.au/spelling_practise_sheet
(also available on page 167)

SET 115

Date: ....

Word List

forgive	**content**	**integrity**	**distinguish**	**cocaine**
location	**explore**	**ethical**	**housing**	**Thanksgiving**
whatever	**society**	**century**	**mistake**	**procedure**

INSTRUCTIONS: Review the word list above and then cover. Have someone read out each word while you write them in the spaces below. Review any misspelt words 3 times.

LOOK. SAY. COVER. WRITE. CHECK.

Practise

Practise 1

Practise 2

Practise 3

TIP Remember, look up each word in your dictionary to learn its meaning!

Need extra practise?
Printable blank practise sheet available from: www.lifelongeducation.com.au/spelling_practise_sheet
(also available on page 167)

SET 116

Date: ....

Word List

appoint	**differently**	**network**	**overlook**	**indigenous**
courage	**evaluate**	**comfortable**	**missionary**	**necessary**
understanding	**landscape**	**athlete**	**surface**	**challenge**

INSTRUCTIONS: Review the word list above and then cover. Have someone read out each word while you write them in the spaces below. Review any misspelt words 3 times.

LOOK. SAY. COVER. WRITE. CHECK.

Practise

Practise 1

Practise 2

Practise 3

TIP Remember, look up each word in your dictionary to learn its meaning!

Need extra practise?
Printable blank practise sheet available from: www.lifelongeducation.com.au/spelling_practise_sheet
(also available on page 167)

SET 117

Date: ....

Word List

receiver	**cottage**	**command**	**illusion**	**valuable**
repeatedly	**garbage**	**ceiling**	**circuit**	**so-called**
suicide	**diagnosis**	**creativity**	**quarter**	**operate**

INSTRUCTIONS: Review the word list above and then cover. Have someone read out each word while you write them in the spaces below. Review any misspelt words 3 times.

LOOK. SAY. COVER. WRITE. CHECK.

Practise

Practise 1

Practise 2

Practise 3

TIP Remember, look up each word in your dictionary to learn its meaning!

Need extra practise?
Printable blank practise sheet available from: www.lifelongeducation.com.au/spelling_practise_sheet
(also available on page 167)

SET 118

Date: ....

Word List

opportunity	**adviser**	**deliberately**	**technician**	**federal**
register	**ability**	**efficiency**	**mixture**	**sustain**
extraordinary	**portfolio**	**conspiracy**	**military**	**commonly**

INSTRUCTIONS: Review the word list above and then cover. Have someone read out each word while you write them in the spaces below. Review any misspelt words 3 times.

LOOK. SAY. COVER. WRITE. CHECK.

Practise

Practise 1

Practise 2

Practise 3

TIP Remember, look up each word in your dictionary to learn its meaning!

Need extra practise?
Printable blank practise sheet available from: www.lifelongeducation.com.au/spelling_practise_sheet (also available on page 167)

SET 119

Date: ....

Word List

develop	**director**	**facility**	**equation**	**outside**
machine	**worldwide**	**psychologist**	**photography**	**beautiful**
ideological	**relative**	**heavily**	**collect**	**accurate**

INSTRUCTIONS: Review the word list above and then cover. Have someone read out each word while you write them in the spaces below. Review any misspelt words 3 times.

LOOK. SAY. COVER. WRITE. CHECK.

Practise

Practise 1

Practise 2

Practise 3

TIP Remember, look up each word in your dictionary to learn its meaning!

Need extra practise?
Printable blank practise sheet available from: www.lifelongeducation.com.au/spelling_practise_sheet
(also available on page 167)

SET 120

Date: ....

Word List

impress	**corporate**	**surprised**	**peaceful**	**decline**
depending	**seminar**	**pretend**	**lecture**	**consumer**
exclusively	**achievement**	**electrical**	**pleasant**	**investigation**

INSTRUCTIONS: Review the word list above and then cover. Have someone read out each word while you write them in the spaces below. Review any misspelt words 3 times.

LOOK. SAY. COVER. WRITE. CHECK.

Practise

Practise 1

Practise 2

Practise 3

TIP Remember, look up each word in your dictionary to learn its meaning!

Need extra practise?
Printable blank practise sheet available from: www.lifelongeducation.com.au/spelling_practise_sheet
(also available on page 167)

SET 121

Date: ....

Word List

physics	**businessman**	**cooperate**	**humanity**	**husband**
welcome	**marketplace**	**marketing**	**indication**	**element**
software	**envision**	**contain**	**tourism**	**regularly**

INSTRUCTIONS: Review the word list above and then cover. Have someone read out each word while you write them in the spaces below. Review any misspelt words 3 times.

LOOK. SAY. COVER. WRITE. CHECK.

Practise

Practise 1

Practise 2

Practise 3

TIP Remember, look up each word in your dictionary to learn its meaning!

Need extra practise?
Printable blank practise sheet available from: www.lifelongeducation.com.au/spelling_practise_sheet
(also available on page 167)

SET 122

Date: ....

Word List

entitle	**placement**	**daughter**	**confuse**	**consent**
surgery	**contribute**	**difference**	**experienced**	**economically**
corporation	**evident**	**consistently**	**interior**	**relatively**

INSTRUCTIONS: Review the word list above and then cover. Have someone read out each word while you write them in the spaces below. Review any misspelt words 3 times.

LOOK. SAY. COVER. WRITE. CHECK.

Practise

Practise 1

Practise 2

Practise 3

TIP Remember, look up each word in your dictionary to learn its meaning!

Need extra practise?
Printable blank practise sheet available from: www.lifelongeducation.com.au/spelling_practise_sheet
(also available on page 167)

SET 123

Date: ....

Word List

landing	**contract**	**vertical**	**preliminary**	**complaint**
confrontation	**eastern**	**opposition**	**intellectual**	**independence**
assembly	**spectrum**	**English**	**context**	**successfully**

INSTRUCTIONS: Review the word list above and then cover. Have someone read out each word while you write them in the spaces below. Review any misspelt words 3 times.

LOOK. SAY. COVER. WRITE. CHECK.

Practise

Practise 1

Practise 2

Practise 3

TIP Remember, look up each word in your dictionary to learn its meaning!

Need extra practise?
Printable blank practise sheet available from: www.lifelongeducation.com.au/spelling_practise_sheet
(also available on page 167)

SET 124

Date: ....

Word List

species	**automobile**	**encounter**	**whenever**	**stimulate**
long-term	**pregnant**	**Olympic**	**hurricane**	**headline**
connect	**breathe**	**two-thirds**	**neutral**	**properly**

INSTRUCTIONS: Review the word list above and then cover. Have someone read out each word while you write them in the spaces below. Review any misspelt words 3 times.

LOOK. SAY. COVER. WRITE. CHECK.

Practise

Practise 1

Practise 2

Practise 3

TIP Remember, look up each word in your dictionary to learn its meaning!

Need extra practise?
Printable blank practise sheet available from: www.lifelongeducation.com.au/spelling_practise_sheet
(also available on page 167)

SET 125

Date: ....

Word List

nonetheless	**approach**	**Chinese**	**grandmother**	**overwhelming**
logical	**burning**	**government**	**profile**	**suddenly**
library	**sequence**	**integration**	**industrial**	**electronic**

INSTRUCTIONS: Review the word list above and then cover. Have someone read out each word while you write them in the spaces below. Review any misspelt words 3 times.

LOOK. SAY. COVER. WRITE. CHECK.

Practise

Practise 1

Practise 2

Practise 3

TIP Remember, look up each word in your dictionary to learn its meaning!

Need extra practise?
Printable blank practise sheet available from: www.lifelongeducation.com.au/spelling_practise_sheet
(also available on page 167)

SET 126

Date: ....

Word List

functional	**message**	**comparison**	**deficit**	**confident**
publicly	**regulation**	**chocolate**	**incident**	**molecule**
consume	**violent**	**encouraging**	**grandchild**	**metaphor**

INSTRUCTIONS: Review the word list above and then cover. Have someone read out each word while you write them in the spaces below. Review any misspelt words 3 times.

LOOK. SAY. COVER. WRITE. CHECK.

Practise

Practise 1

Practise 2

Practise 3

TIP Remember, look up each word in your dictionary to learn its meaning!

Need extra practise?
Printable blank practise sheet available from: www.lifelongeducation.com.au/spelling_practise_sheet
(also available on page 167)

SET 127

Date: ....

Word List

treatment	**present**	**dynamics**	**researcher**	**bedroom**
authority	**correctly**	**obstacle**	**guarantee**	**deserve**
science	**assumption**	**transformation**	**funeral**	**remember**

INSTRUCTIONS: Review the word list above and then cover. Have someone read out each word while you write them in the spaces below. Review any misspelt words 3 times.

LOOK. SAY. COVER. WRITE. CHECK.

Practise

Practise 1

Practise 2

Practise 3

TIP Remember, look up each word in your dictionary to learn its meaning!

Need extra practise?
Printable blank practise sheet available from: www.lifelongeducation.com.au/spelling_practise_sheet
(also available on page 167)

SET 128

Date: ....

Word List

organizational	**shoulder**	**between**	**feeling**	**blessing**
workout	**missing**	**pleased**	**industry**	**clothing**
thinking	**democracy**	**occasional**	**diversity**	**sibling**

INSTRUCTIONS: Review the word list above and then cover. Have someone read out each word while you write them in the spaces below. Review any misspelt words 3 times.

LOOK. SAY. COVER. WRITE. CHECK.

Practise

Practise 1

Practise 2

Practise 3

TIP Remember, look up each word in your dictionary to learn its meaning!

Need extra practise?
Printable blank practise sheet available from: www.lifelongeducation.com.au/spelling_practise_sheet
(also available on page 167)

SET 129

Date: ....

Word List

definition	**operation**	**collaboration**	**questionnaire**	**perfectly**
opponent	**confession**	**station**	**furniture**	**historian**
business	**legitimate**	**exclude**	**endless**	**vegetable**

INSTRUCTIONS: Review the word list above and then cover. Have someone read out each word while you write them in the spaces below. Review any misspelt words 3 times.

LOOK. SAY. COVER. WRITE. CHECK.

Practise

Practise 1

Practise 2

Practise 3

TIP Remember, look up each word in your dictionary to learn its meaning!

Need extra practise?
Printable blank practise sheet available from: www.lifelongeducation.com.au/spelling_practise_sheet
(also available on page 167)

SET 130

Date: ....

Word List

occasion	**barrier**	**section**	**cemetery**	**alternative**
successful	**protest**	**prosecution**	**transition**	**contractor**
detailed	**approval**	**religious**	**failure**	**introduction**

INSTRUCTIONS: Review the word list above and then cover. Have someone read out each word while you write them in the spaces below. Review any misspelt words 3 times.

LOOK. SAY. COVER. WRITE. CHECK.

Practise

Practise 1

Practise 2

Practise 3

TIP Remember, look up each word in your dictionary to learn its meaning!

Need extra practise?
Printable blank practise sheet available from: www.lifelongeducation.com.au/spelling_practise_sheet
(also available on page 167)

SET 131

Date: ....

Word List

embarrassed	**laboratory**	**articulate**	**examination**	**remaining**
monitor	**psychology**	**presence**	**campaign**	**excessive**
knowledge	**protect**	**Internet**	**swallow**	**commissioner**

INSTRUCTIONS: Review the word list above and then cover. Have someone read out each word while you write them in the spaces below. Review any misspelt words 3 times.

LOOK. SAY. COVER. WRITE. CHECK.

Practise

Practise 1

Practise 2

Practise 3

TIP Remember, look up each word in your dictionary to learn its meaning!

Need extra practise?
Printable blank practise sheet available from: www.lifelongeducation.com.au/spelling_practise_sheet
(also available on page 167)

SET 132

Date: ....

Word List

accompany	**conviction**	**conflict**	**nightmare**	**numerous**
altogether	**adolescent**	**perhaps**	**visible**	**consult**
limitation	**bacteria**	**donation**	**conventional**	**interested**

INSTRUCTIONS: Review the word list above and then cover. Have someone read out each word while you write them in the spaces below. Review any misspelt words 3 times.

LOOK. SAY. COVER. WRITE. CHECK.

Practise

Practise 1

Practise 2

Practise 3

TIP Remember, look up each word in your dictionary to learn its meaning!

Need extra practise?
Printable blank practise sheet available from: www.lifelongeducation.com.au/spelling_practise_sheet
(also available on page 167)

SET 133

Date: ....

Word List

realise	**reliability**	**historic**	**Canadian**	**decrease**
uncomfortable	**dancing**	**celebrate**	**dilemma**	**overcome**
accident	**withdraw**	**influential**	**representation**	**miracle**

INSTRUCTIONS: Review the word list above and then cover. Have someone read out each word while you write them in the spaces below. Review any misspelt words 3 times.

LOOK. SAY. COVER. WRITE. CHECK.

Practise

Practise 1

Practise 2

Practise 3

TIP Remember, look up each word in your dictionary to learn its meaning!

Need extra practise?
Printable blank practise sheet available from: www.lifelongeducation.com.au/spelling_practise_sheet
(also available on page 167)

SET 134

Date: ....

Word List

somehow	**embrace**	**pollution**	**publicity**	**transportation**
discuss	**additional**	**acquisition**	**officer**	**comprise**
commission	**charter**	**technological**	**setting**	**marriage**

INSTRUCTIONS: Review the word list above and then cover. Have someone read out each word while you write them in the spaces below. Review any misspelt words 3 times.

LOOK. SAY. COVER. WRITE. CHECK.

Practise

Practise 1

Practise 2

Practise 3

TIP Remember, look up each word in your dictionary to learn its meaning!

Need extra practise?
Printable blank practise sheet available from: www.lifelongeducation.com.au/spelling_practise_sheet
(also available on page 167)

SET 135

Date: ....

Word List

everyone	**anywhere**	**devastating**	**variety**	**quantity**
equivalent	**economic**	**airline**	**attractive**	**credibility**
increased	**resident**	**journalism**	**counterpart**	**working**

INSTRUCTIONS: Review the word list above and then cover. Have someone read out each word while you write them in the spaces below. Review any misspelt words 3 times.

LOOK. SAY. COVER. WRITE. CHECK.

Practise

Practise 1

Practise 2

Practise 3

TIP Remember, look up each word in your dictionary to learn its meaning!

Need extra practise?
Printable blank practise sheet available from: www.lifelongeducation.com.au/spelling_practise_sheet
(also available on page 167)

SET 136

Date: ....

Word List

frankly	**willingness**	**efficient**	**mention**	**Catholic**
instinct	**participation**	**assistance**	**accusation**	**strongly**
convert	**criminal**	**exclusive**	**internal**	**however**

INSTRUCTIONS: Review the word list above and then cover. Have someone read out each word while you write them in the spaces below. Review any misspelt words 3 times.

LOOK. SAY. COVER. WRITE. CHECK.

Practise

Practise 1

Practise 2

Practise 3

TIP Remember, look up each word in your dictionary to learn its meaning!

Need extra practise?
Printable blank practise sheet available from: www.lifelongeducation.com.au/spelling_practise_sheet
(also available on page 167)

SET 137

Date: ....

Word List

premium	**commander**	**descend**	**epidemic**	**validity**
discount	**occupation**	**statement**	**attempt**	**encourage**
minimise	**indicator**	**greatest**	**sunlight**	**nuclear**

INSTRUCTIONS: Review the word list above and then cover. Have someone read out each word while you write them in the spaces below. Review any misspelt words 3 times.

LOOK. SAY. COVER. WRITE. CHECK.

Practise

Practise 1

Practise 2

Practise 3

TIP Remember, look up each word in your dictionary to learn its meaning!

Need extra practise?
Printable blank practise sheet available from: www.lifelongeducation.com.au/spelling_practise_sheet
(also available on page 167)

SET 138

Date: ....

Word List

estimate	**consecutive**	**offense**	**patient**	**prohibit**
special	**philosophy**	**publish**	**replacement**	**rational**
introduce	**domestic**	**tourist**	**running**	**Australia**

INSTRUCTIONS: Review the word list above and then cover. Have someone read out each word while you write them in the spaces below. Review any misspelt words 3 times.

LOOK. SAY. COVER. WRITE. CHECK.

Practise

Practise 1

Practise 2

Practise 3

TIP Remember, look up each word in your dictionary to learn its meaning!

Need extra practise?
Printable blank practise sheet available from: www.lifelongeducation.com.au/spelling_practise_sheet
(also available on page 167)

SET 139

Date: ....

Word List

Saturday	**Thursday**	**Wednesday**	**Tuesday**	**Adelaide**
Melbourne	**Brisbane**	**Victoria**	**homogenise**	**somersault**
feasible	**illiterate**	**jeopardise**	**lieutenant**	**landslide**

INSTRUCTIONS: Review the word list above and then cover. Have someone read out each word while you write them in the spaces below. Review any misspelt words 3 times.

LOOK. SAY. COVER. WRITE. CHECK.

Practise

Practise 1

Practise 2

Practise 3

TIP Remember, look up each word in your dictionary to learn its meaning!

Need extra practise?
Printable blank practise sheet available from: www.lifelongeducation.com.au/spelling_practise_sheet
(also available on page 167)

SET 140

Date: ....

Word List

oregano	**aversion**	**obstinate**	**microcosm**	**unwilling**
commuter	**burglar**	**mobilise**	**invalid**	**skeptical**
jeopardy	**caution**	**classification**	**mispronounce**	**studies**

INSTRUCTIONS: Review the word list above and then cover. Have someone read out each word while you write them in the spaces below. Review any misspelt words 3 times.

LOOK. SAY. COVER. WRITE. CHECK.

Practise

Practise 1

Practise 2

Practise 3

TIP Remember, look up each word in your dictionary to learn its meaning!

Need extra practise?

Printable blank practise sheet available from: www.lifelongeducation.com.au/spelling_practise_sheet (also available on page 167)

SET 141

Date: ....

Word List

preferred	**precipice**	**absorbent**	**recurring**	**liaison**
impatient	**statutory**	**diffidence**	**inferior**	**warranty**
skillet	**repulse**	**treachery**	**banquet**	**emulate**

INSTRUCTIONS: Review the word list above and then cover. Have someone read out each word while you write them in the spaces below. Review any misspelt words 3 times.

LOOK. SAY. COVER. WRITE. CHECK.

Practise

Practise 1

Practise 2

Practise 3

TIP Remember, look up each word in your dictionary to learn its meaning!

Need extra practise?
Printable blank practise sheet available from: www.lifelongeducation.com.au/spelling_practise_sheet
(also available on page 167)

SET 142

Date: ....

Word List

futurity	**semester**	**malicious**	**collateral**	**duplicate**
turmoil	**stopped**	**obnoxious**	**disappeared**	**rainstorm**
clientele	**distress**	**appliance**	**desecration**	**cartage**

INSTRUCTIONS: Review the word list above and then cover. Have someone read out each word while you write them in the spaces below. Review any misspelt words 3 times.

LOOK. SAY. COVER. WRITE. CHECK.

Practise

Practise 1

Practise 2

Practise 3

TIP Remember, look up each word in your dictionary to learn its meaning!

Need extra practise?
Printable blank practise sheet available from: www.lifelongeducation.com.au/spelling_practise_sheet
(also available on page 167)

SET 143

Date: ....

Word List

loophole	**insinuate**	**cafeteria**	**indelible**	**noticeable**
sculptor	**simplicity**	**imbecile**	**indulge**	**grabbed**
extricate	**kindergarten**	**understood**	**rapacious**	**accessory**

INSTRUCTIONS: Review the word list above and then cover. Have someone read out each word while you write them in the spaces below. Review any misspelt words 3 times.

LOOK. SAY. COVER. WRITE. CHECK.

Practise

Practise 1

Practise 2

Practise 3

TIP Remember, look up each word in your dictionary to learn its meaning!

Need extra practise?
Printable blank practise sheet available from: www.lifelongeducation.com.au/spelling_practise_sheet
(also available on page 167)

SET 144

Date: ....

Word List

scarcely	**oneself**	**critique**	**further**	**harness**
imitation	**underwear**	**strenuous**	**tyranny**	**magnify**
volcano	**despoil**	**nuisance**	**fearless**	**petition**

INSTRUCTIONS: Review the word list above and then cover. Have someone read out each word while you write them in the spaces below. Review any misspelt words 3 times.

LOOK. SAY. COVER. WRITE. CHECK.

Practise

Practise 1

Practise 2

Practise 3

TIP Remember, look up each word in your dictionary to learn its meaning!

Need extra practise?
Printable blank practise sheet available from: www.lifelongeducation.com.au/spelling_practise_sheet
(also available on page 167)

SET 145

Date: ....

Word List

mercurial	**benefited**	**scarecrow**	**ailment**	**chauffeur**
fastidious	**lunchroom**	**paradoxical**	**fortress**	**televise**
volleyball	**doghouse**	**directory**	**misgiving**	**anecdote**

INSTRUCTIONS: Review the word list above and then cover. Have someone read out each word while you write them in the spaces below. Review any misspelt words 3 times.

LOOK. SAY. COVER. WRITE. CHECK.

Practise

Practise 1

Practise 2

Practise 3

TIP Remember, look up each word in your dictionary to learn its meaning!

Need extra practise?
Printable blank practise sheet available from: www.lifelongeducation.com.au/spelling_practise_sheet
(also available on page 167)

SET 146

Date: ....

Word List

civilise	**acquittal**	**awkward**	**spelling**	**attorneys**
discrepancy	**mattress**	**perseverance**	**folklore**	**ransack**
facsimile	**beginner**	**plantation**	**centigram**	**capitalization**

INSTRUCTIONS: Review the word list above and then cover. Have someone read out each word while you write them in the spaces below. Review any misspelt words 3 times.

LOOK. SAY. COVER. WRITE. CHECK.

Practise

Practise 1

Practise 2

Practise 3

TIP Remember, look up each word in your dictionary to learn its meaning!

Need extra practise?
Printable blank practise sheet available from: www.lifelongeducation.com.au/spelling_practise_sheet
(also available on page 167)

SET 147

Date: ....

Word List

unaware	**metallic**	**aviator**	**kerosene**	**misunderstood**
poignancy	**jellyfish**	**descent**	**incandescent**	**pretzel**
forfeit	**asphalt**	**bulletin**	**calculator**	**entertain**

INSTRUCTIONS: Review the word list above and then cover. Have someone read out each word while you write them in the spaces below. Review any misspelt words 3 times.

LOOK. SAY. COVER. WRITE. CHECK.

Practise

Practise 1

Practise 2

Practise 3

TIP Remember, look up each word in your dictionary to learn its meaning!

Need extra practise?
Printable blank practise sheet available from: www.lifelongeducation.com.au/spelling_practise_sheet
(also available on page 167)

SET 148

Date: ....

Word List

junction	**picnicking**	**prospectus**	**extravagant**	**durable**
solitary	**antidote**	**periodical**	**forcible**	**sleight**
dominance	**cylinder**	**guardian**	**shuffle**	**crystallise**

INSTRUCTIONS: Review the word list above and then cover. Have someone read out each word while you write them in the spaces below. Review any misspelt words 3 times.

LOOK. SAY. COVER. WRITE. CHECK.

Practise

Practise 1

Practise 2

Practise 3

TIP Remember, look up each word in your dictionary to learn its meaning!

Need extra practise?
Printable blank practise sheet available from: www.lifelongeducation.com.au/spelling_practise_sheet
(also available on page 167)

SET 149

Date: ....

Word List

advertisement	**nonfiction**	**medicinal**	**notoriety**	**disposition**
innumerable	**Mercury**	**mightily**	**daylight**	**kindness**
allotted	**nucleus**	**bondage**	**frivolous**	**gaseous**

INSTRUCTIONS: Review the word list above and then cover. Have someone read out each word while you write them in the spaces below. Review any misspelt words 3 times.

LOOK. SAY. COVER. WRITE. CHECK.

Practise

Practise 1

Practise 2

Practise 3

TIP Remember, look up each word in your dictionary to learn its meaning!

Need extra practise?
Printable blank practise sheet available from: www.lifelongeducation.com.au/spelling_practise_sheet
(also available on page 167)

SET 150

Date: ....

Word List

buffalo	**inquire**	**disapprove**	**playground**	**insecure**
gorgeous	**poignant**	**accompanied**	**ecstasy**	**evanescent**
besieged	**lettuce**	**newsstand**	**cabbage**	**decorator**

INSTRUCTIONS: Review the word list above and then cover. Have someone read out each word while you write them in the spaces below. Review any misspelt words 3 times.

LOOK. SAY. COVER. WRITE. CHECK.

Practise

Practise 1

Practise 2

Practise 3

TIP Remember, look up each word in your dictionary to learn its meaning!

Need extra practise?
Printable blank practise sheet available from: www.lifelongeducation.com.au/spelling_practise_sheet
(also available on page 167)

SET 151

Date: ....

Word List

withhold	**flamboyant**	**embarrass**	**trousers**	**cancellation**
tornado	**saturate**	**railway**	**evidently**	**manuscript**
cinnamon	**crouton**	**tangible**	**thieves**	**incautious**

INSTRUCTIONS: Review the word list above and then cover. Have someone read out each word while you write them in the spaces below. Review any misspelt words 3 times.

LOOK. SAY. COVER. WRITE. CHECK.

Practise

Practise 1

Practise 2

Practise 3

TIP Remember, look up each word in your dictionary to learn its meaning!

Need extra practise?
Printable blank practise sheet available from: www.lifelongeducation.com.au/spelling_practise_sheet
(also available on page 167)

SET 152

Date: ....

Word List

dissociate	**kangaroo**	**officious**	**equilibrium**	**barbecue**
goldfish	**numerator**	**hygiene**	**laborer**	**foolish**
roommate	**wrestle**	**equipping**	**janitor**	**insoluble**

INSTRUCTIONS: Review the word list above and then cover. Have someone read out each word while you write them in the spaces below. Review any misspelt words 3 times.

LOOK. SAY. COVER. WRITE. CHECK.

Practise

Practise 1

Practise 2

Practise 3

TIP Remember, look up each word in your dictionary to learn its meaning!

Need extra practise?
Printable blank practise sheet available from: www.lifelongeducation.com.au/spelling_practise_sheet
(also available on page 167)

SET 153

Date: ....

Word List

gnawing	**commerce**	**unacceptable**	**innocence**	**escapade**
haircut	**plethora**	**squirrel**	**anachronism**	**pamphlet**
disposal	**aftermath**	**delegate**	**unmoved**	**boycott**

INSTRUCTIONS: Review the word list above and then cover. Have someone read out each word while you write them in the spaces below. Review any misspelt words 3 times.

LOOK. SAY. COVER. WRITE. CHECK.

Practise

Practise 1

Practise 2

Practise 3

TIP Remember, look up each word in your dictionary to learn its meaning!

Need extra practise?
Printable blank practise sheet available from: www.lifelongeducation.com.au/spelling_practise_sheet
(also available on page 167)

SET 154

Date: ....

Word List

sincerely	**admissible**	**reconcile**	**salvation**	**willful**
expenditure	**shutter**	**thoroughbred**	**naughty**	**opossum**
extract	**angular**	**turpitud**	**amorous**	**colander**

INSTRUCTIONS: Review the word list above and then cover. Have someone read out each word while you write them in the spaces below. Review any misspelt words 3 times.

LOOK. SAY. COVER. WRITE. CHECK.

Practise

Practise 1

Practise 2

Practise 3

TIP Remember, look up each word in your dictionary to learn its meaning!

Need extra practise?
Printable blank practise sheet available from: www.lifelongeducation.com.au/spelling_practise_sheet
(also available on page 167)

SET 155

Date: ....

Word List

preoccupy	**nonentity**	**friction**	**contiguous**	**humidor**
dishonest	**brilliance**	**pastime**	**sanctuary**	**depreciation**
valiant	**delinquent**	**acknowledgment**	**antique**	**competent**

INSTRUCTIONS: Review the word list above and then cover. Have someone read out each word while you write them in the spaces below. Review any misspelt words 3 times.

LOOK. SAY. COVER. WRITE. CHECK.

Practise

Practise 1

Practise 2

Practise 3

TIP Remember, look up each word in your dictionary to learn its meaning!

Need extra practise?
Printable blank practise sheet available from: www.lifelongeducation.com.au/spelling_practise_sheet
(also available on page 167)

SET 156

Date: ....

Word List

passable	**advisor**	**diurnal**	**vengeance**	**brightly**
nineteen	**apparel**	**manageable**	**idiosyncrasy**	**hobbies**
irrevocable	**arguing**	**sedition**	**daybreak**	**berserk**

INSTRUCTIONS: Review the word list above and then cover. Have someone read out each word while you write them in the spaces below. Review any misspelt words 3 times.

LOOK. SAY. COVER. WRITE. CHECK.

Practise

Practise 1

Practise 2

Practise 3

TIP Remember, look up each word in your dictionary to learn its meaning!

Need extra practise?
Printable blank practise sheet available from: www.lifelongeducation.com.au/spelling_practise_sheet
(also available on page 167)

SET 157

Date: ....

Word List

quandary	**farther**	**baritone**	**detrimental**	**lacquer**
horrific	**stepped**	**raccoon**	**receipt**	**haphazard**
irrefutable	**paucity**	**silhouette**	**mileage**	**judicious**

INSTRUCTIONS: Review the word list above and then cover. Have someone read out each word while you write them in the spaces below. Review any misspelt words 3 times.

LOOK. SAY. COVER. WRITE. CHECK.

Practise

Practise 1

Practise 2

Practise 3

TIP Remember, look up each word in your dictionary to learn its meaning!

Need extra practise?
Printable blank practise sheet available from: www.lifelongeducation.com.au/spelling_practise_sheet
(also available on page 167)

SET 158

Date: ....

Word List

testimonial	**varnish**	**catastrophe**	**grotesque**	**mischievous**
disbursement	**enslave**	**vagrant**	**limestone**	**handkerchief**
alchemy	**obligate**	**oblique**	**menthol**	**jealous**

INSTRUCTIONS: Review the word list above and then cover. Have someone read out each word while you write them in the spaces below. Review any misspelt words 3 times.

LOOK. SAY. COVER. WRITE. CHECK.

Practise

Practise 1

Practise 2

Practise 3

TIP Remember, look up each word in your dictionary to learn its meaning!

Need extra practise?
Printable blank practise sheet available from: www.lifelongeducation.com.au/spelling_practise_sheet
(also available on page 167)

SET 159

Date: ....

Word List

domesticate	**handicapped**	**preschool**	**adjourn**	**irksome**
afterthought	**imitate**	**itemised**	**helpless**	**leisure**
immovable	**geology**	**secretarial**	**eminent**	**gigantic**

INSTRUCTIONS: Review the word list above and then cover. Have someone read out each word while you write them in the spaces below. Review any misspelt words 3 times.

LOOK. SAY. COVER. WRITE. CHECK.

Practise

Practise 1

Practise 2

Practise 3

TIP Remember, look up each word in your dictionary to learn its meaning!

Need extra practise?
Printable blank practise sheet available from: www.lifelongeducation.com.au/spelling_practise_sheet
(also available on page 167)

SET 160

Date: ....

Word List

customary	**prostrate**	**predecessor**	**mesmerise**	**extremity**
narrate	**overrate**	**devotion**	**freight**	**earnest**
inflate	**barbaric**	**perspire**	**subvert**	**culprit**

INSTRUCTIONS: Review the word list above and then cover. Have someone read out each word while you write them in the spaces below. Review any misspelt words 3 times.

LOOK. SAY. COVER. WRITE. CHECK.

Practise

Practise 1

Practise 2

Practise 3

TIP Remember, look up each word in your dictionary to learn its meaning!

Need extra practise?
Printable blank practise sheet available from: www.lifelongeducation.com.au/spelling_practise_sheet
(also available on page 167)

SET 161

Date: ....

Word List

encouragement	**prairie**	**giraffe**	**handling**	**infinite**
erroneous	**monologue**	**amphibian**	**imbalance**	**prejudice**
Parliament	**insistent**	**intelligible**	**gymnasium**	**retrieve**

INSTRUCTIONS: Review the word list above and then cover. Have someone read out each word while you write them in the spaces below. Review any misspelt words 3 times.

LOOK. SAY. COVER. WRITE. CHECK.

Practise

Practise 1

Practise 2

Practise 3

TIP Remember, look up each word in your dictionary to learn its meaning!

Need extra practise?
Printable blank practise sheet available from: www.lifelongeducation.com.au/spelling_practise_sheet
(also available on page 167)

SET 162

Date: ....

Word List

misfortune	**fluorescent**	**malefactor**	**furious**	**scissors**
modicum	**illustration**	**chimney**	**mailbox**	**inconsolable**
hopeless	**altercation**	**honorary**	**antiseptic**	**arithmetic**

INSTRUCTIONS: Review the word list above and then cover. Have someone read out each word while you write them in the spaces below. Review any misspelt words 3 times.

LOOK. SAY. COVER. WRITE. CHECK.

Practise

Practise 1

Practise 2

Practise 3

TIP Remember, look up each word in your dictionary to learn its meaning!

Need extra practise?
Printable blank practise sheet available from: www.lifelongeducation.com.au/spelling_practise_sheet
(also available on page 167)

SET 163

Date: ....

Word List

transmutation	**obsolete**	**flourish**	**cologne**	**interrogative**
submarine	**quixotic**	**schooner**	**fulfill**	**hazardous**
surmount	**voucher**	**careless**	**issuing**	**frostbitten**

INSTRUCTIONS: Review the word list above and then cover. Have someone read out each word while you write them in the spaces below. Review any misspelt words 3 times.

LOOK. SAY. COVER. WRITE. CHECK.

Practise

Practise 1

Practise 2

Practise 3

TIP Remember, look up each word in your dictionary to learn its meaning!

Need extra practise?
Printable blank practise sheet available from: www.lifelongeducation.com.au/spelling_practise_sheet
(also available on page 167)

SET 164

Date: ....

Word List

accidentally	**contrary**	**nondescript**	**comical**	**desolate**
galling	**strident**	**camouflage**	**disapproval**	**affects**
option,overrule	**allotment**	**radioactive**	**medallion**	**unnecessary**

INSTRUCTIONS: Review the word list above and then cover. Have someone read out each word while you write them in the spaces below. Review any misspelt words 3 times.

LOOK. SAY. COVER. WRITE. CHECK.

Practise

Practise 1

Practise 2

Practise 3

TIP Remember, look up each word in your dictionary to learn its meaning!

Need extra practise?
Printable blank practise sheet available from: www.lifelongeducation.com.au/spelling_practise_sheet
(also available on page 167)

SET 165

Date: ....

Word List

centripetal	**pavilion**	**factual**	**tearful**	**belittle**
poultry	**imaginary**	**sailboat**	**recluse**	**intensify**
hosiery	**obedience**	**abolish**	**memorable**	**negligence**

INSTRUCTIONS: Review the word list above and then cover. Have someone read out each word while you write them in the spaces below. Review any misspelt words 3 times.

LOOK. SAY. COVER. WRITE. CHECK.

Practise

Practise 1

Practise 2

Practise 3

TIP Remember, look up each word in your dictionary to learn its meaning!

Need extra practise?
Printable blank practise sheet available from: www.lifelongeducation.com.au/spelling_practise_sheet
(also available on page 167)

SET 166

Date: ....

Word List

mistreat	**brochure**	**budgeting**	**materialism**	**cheddar**
microbe	**dormitory**	**recreation**	**desirable**	**seminary**
capricious	**disguise**	**wholesale**	**glacier**	**impatience**

INSTRUCTIONS: Review the word list above and then cover. Have someone read out each word while you write them in the spaces below. Review any misspelt words 3 times.

LOOK. SAY. COVER. WRITE. CHECK.

Practise

Practise 1

Practise 2

Practise 3

TIP Remember, look up each word in your dictionary to learn its meaning!

Need extra practise?
Printable blank practise sheet available from: www.lifelongeducation.com.au/spelling_practise_sheet
(also available on page 167)

SET 167

Date: ....

Word List

disoblige	**exceptional**	**canvass**	**rapport**	**elliptical**
measles	**vinegar**	**discernible**	**expediency**	**submission**
deficient	**dehydration**	**expedite**	**invariable**	**carpenter**

INSTRUCTIONS: Review the word list above and then cover. Have someone read out each word while you write them in the spaces below. Review any misspelt words 3 times.

LOOK. SAY. COVER. WRITE. CHECK.

Practise

Practise 1

Practise 2

Practise 3

TIP Remember, look up each word in your dictionary to learn its meaning!

Need extra practise?
Printable blank practise sheet available from: www.lifelongeducation.com.au/spelling_practise_sheet
(also available on page 167)

SET 168

Date: ....

Word List

transient	**surfeit**	**corporal**	**monotonous**	**pronounce**
counterfeit	**underdog**	**asterisk**	**raucous**	**zoology**
soprano	**milking**	**preceding**	**miniature**	**visiting**

INSTRUCTIONS: Review the word list above and then cover. Have someone read out each word while you write them in the spaces below. Review any misspelt words 3 times.

LOOK. SAY. COVER. WRITE. CHECK.

Practise

Practise 1

Practise 2

Practise 3

TIP Remember, look up each word in your dictionary to learn its meaning!

Need extra practise?
Printable blank practise sheet available from: www.lifelongeducation.com.au/spelling_practise_sheet
(also available on page 167)

SET 169

Date: ....

Word List

toothpaste	**creditor**	**inscription**	**fertile**	**ladybug**
impinge	**didactic**	**presage**	**mosquito**	**hydrant**
luncheon	**caption**	**scrabble**	**abbreviate**	**disinterested**

INSTRUCTIONS: Review the word list above and then cover. Have someone read out each word while you write them in the spaces below. Review any misspelt words 3 times.

LOOK. SAY. COVER. WRITE. CHECK.

Practise

Practise 1

Practise 2

Practise 3

TIP Remember, look up each word in your dictionary to learn its meaning!

Need extra practise?
Printable blank practise sheet available from: www.lifelongeducation.com.au/spelling_practise_sheet
(also available on page 167)

SET 170

Date: ....

Word List

maneuver	**calligraphy**	**teachable**	**algebra**	**laborious**
perforated	**recitation**	**inaugural**	**labeling**	**recline**
serviceable	**obesity**	**syllable**	**justifiable**	**scholastic**

INSTRUCTIONS: Review the word list above and then cover. Have someone read out each word while you write them in the spaces below. Review any misspelt words 3 times.

LOOK. SAY. COVER. WRITE. CHECK.

Practise

Practise 1

Practise 2

Practise 3

TIP Remember, look up each word in your dictionary to learn its meaning!

Need extra practise?
Printable blank practise sheet available from: www.lifelongeducation.com.au/spelling_practise_sheet
(also available on page 167)

SET 171

Date: ....

Word List

keyboard	**kilometre**	**determined**	**diagram**	**licence**
lunchtime	**machinery**	**disappoint**	**favourite**	**confine**
disgusting	**confusing**	**medieval**	**millimetre**	**firstly**

INSTRUCTIONS: Review the word list above and then cover. Have someone read out each word while you write them in the spaces below. Review any misspelt words 3 times.

LOOK. SAY. COVER. WRITE. CHECK.

Practise

Practise 1

Practise 2

Practise 3

TIP Remember, look up each word in your dictionary to learn its meaning!

Need extra practise?
Printable blank practise sheet available from: www.lifelongeducation.com.au/spelling_practise_sheet
(also available on page 167)

SET 172

Date: ....

Word List

flavour	**formally**	**fortunate**	**motorway**	**freeway**
centimetre	**freezer**	**downstairs**	**frightened**	**neighbour**
beforehand	**neighbourhood**	**nonsense**	**nowadays**	**goodness**

INSTRUCTIONS: Review the word list above and then cover. Have someone read out each word while you write them in the spaces below. Review any misspelt words 3 times.

LOOK. SAY. COVER. WRITE. CHECK.

Practise

Practise 1

Practise 2

Practise 3

TIP Remember, look up each word in your dictionary to learn its meaning!

Need extra practise?

Printable blank practise sheet available from: www.lifelongeducation.com.au/spelling_practise_sheet (also available on page 167)

SET 173

Date: ....

Word List

grammar	**offence**	**grandpa**	**behaviour**	**holding**
overseas	**ideally**	**overtime**	**countryside**	**criterion**
boiling	**conscientious**	**cushion**	**biscuit**	**subsequently**

INSTRUCTIONS: Review the word list above and then cover. Have someone read out each word while you write them in the spaces below. Review any misspelt words 3 times.

LOOK. SAY. COVER. WRITE. CHECK.

Practise

Practise 1

Practise 2

Practise 3

TIP Remember, look up each word in your dictionary to learn its meaning!

Need extra practise?
Printable blank practise sheet available from: www.lifelongeducation.com.au/spelling_practise_sheet
(also available on page 167)

SET 174

Date: ....

Word List

conspicuous	**laryngitis**	**liquorice**	**convenient**	**predeterminer**
ashamed	**gravity**	**congratulations**	**ghastly**	**phantom**
gracious	**regime**	**bizarre**	**gherkin**	**fiasco**

INSTRUCTIONS: Review the word list above and then cover. Have someone read out each word while you write them in the spaces below. Review any misspelt words 3 times.

LOOK. SAY. COVER. WRITE. CHECK.

Practise

Practise 1

Practise 2

Practise 3

TIP Remember, look up each word in your dictionary to learn its meaning!

Need extra practise?
Printable blank practise sheet available from: www.lifelongeducation.com.au/spelling_practise_sheet (also available on page 167)

APPENDIX

PRACTISE SHEET

Lifelong Education
www.lifelongeducation.com.au

Practise 1

Practise 2

Practise 3

Practise 4

Practise 5

Practise 6

Made in the USA
Coppell, TX
04 November 2026

11263981R00101